Happt
birthday
darling!

Claire
xxxx

one woman walking

from fear to freedom

by joanne elizabeth moore

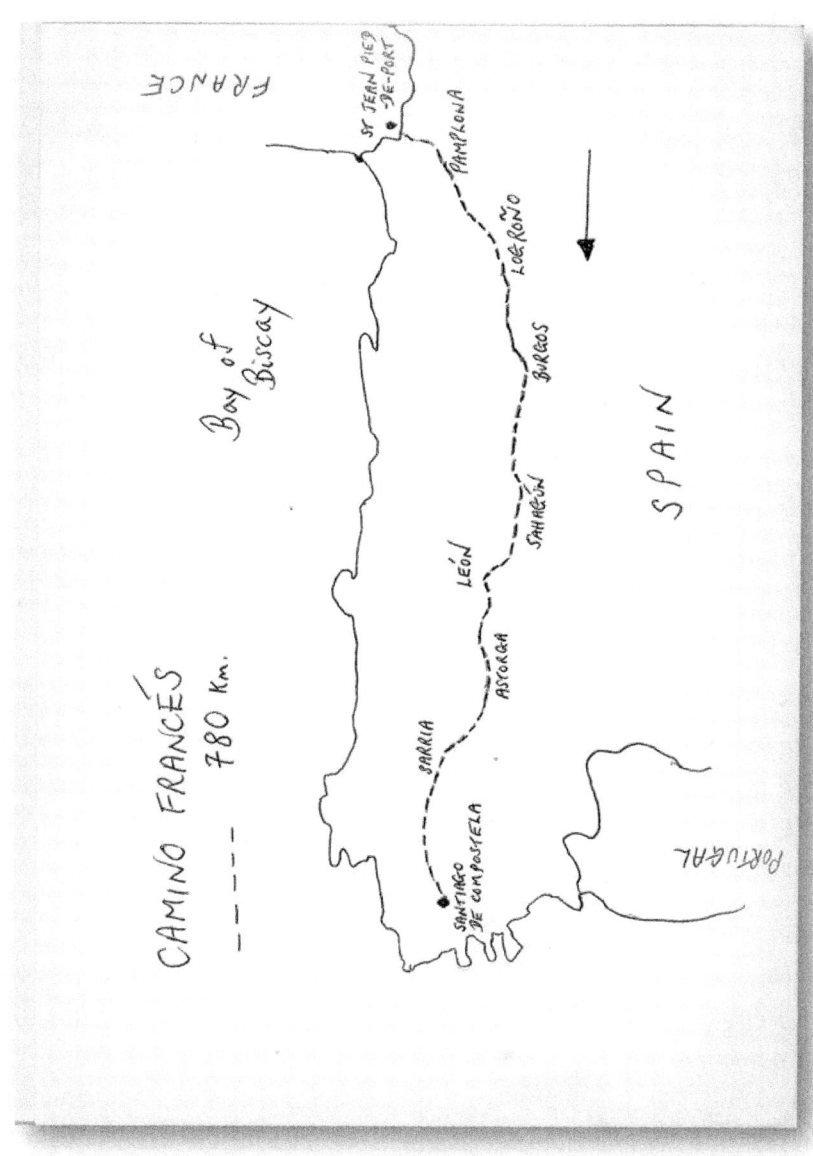

CAMINO FRANCÉS
---- 780 Km.

FRANCE

ST JEAN PIED DE-PORT
PAMPLONA
LOGROÑO
BURGOS
SAHAGÚN
LEÓN
ASTORGA
BARRIA
SANTIAGO DE COMPOSTELA

Bay of Biscay

SPAIN

PORTUGAL

Acknowledgements

All the people I want to thank for their help and encouragement in putting this book together already know how grateful I am and so I don't need to make a long list of individual acknowledgements. But there are four people to whom I do want to give a special mention.

The first is my niece, Hannah, who at the tender age of thirteen advised me not to get too serious as I got older. Thank you, Hannah, for your excellent advice. I try to smile and laugh every day and I hope you do too.

The second person is a friend of a friend called Sarah, a retired headmistress, whom I met several years ago and was the first person to tell me to knuckle down and write this book. Thank you, Sarah, I hope you like it.

The third is a dear friend, John Murphy, who is always the first person I can call on to critique a book, honestly and without prejudice. In an age where we are all always so busy, John gives his times so graciously to do this for myself and for others and words of gratitude are simply not enough. But thank you, John, from the bottom of my heart.

The fourth is a much respected and admired author of mine, Eleanor O'Hanlon, who has written the most amazingly, beautiful book I have ever read. Her words and style are elegant, carry poignancy and demand attention in every paragraph that she writes. Not only have I been inspired by her written words but Eleanor also spent a lot of her valuable time - beyond my wildest expectations! - encouraging me to improve this book, its core threads and content. I cannot express my gratitude enough, Eleanor. I hope you like it too.

…/…

Table of Contents

Preamble

Early one morning in mid-March 2015, I was stood in an *albergue* kitchen in northern Spain, looking out of the dirty window into a rain-splashed and drab, cloud-blackened street in Triacastela, waiting for the light to grow just a little bit more before I set out on that day's leg of the Camino de Santiago. I raised an eyebrow as I heard a rare, early morning riser enter the kitchen behind me. Undoubtedly Spanish at this hour. Only the Spanish and I got up so early. We quietly shared our *holas* and I returned to pondering whether the rain was going to stop, just for once, on this hitherto bleak and cold Camino trek or whether I would once again be wearing my plastic poncho in an attempt to fend off torrential downpours over the next ten hours.

Unexpectedly, the fellow walker cleared his throat and asked me if I was English. By his accent I could tell he was Spanish. I turned and saw the serious, brown face of a weather-beaten man in his late fifties. I said yes. He then asked me if I walked alone. Again, I said yes. He asked me how far I was walking each day. I replied anywhere between thirty-five and forty kilometres. He looked me dead in the eye before, quite suddenly, he burst into a broad smile and then proceeded to ask me if he could shake my hand. I smiled wryly and wondered which detail in particular had caught his imagination. My mind filled with a kaleidoscope of visuals from the past two weeks: sometimes walking bent over double into the relentless, westerly wind; many times soaked to the skin and freezing, screaming aloud my curses up to the heavens as I stomped my way through four hours of unyielding rain; clumsily trudging through two foot of fresh, crispy, untouched snow up and down both sides of O'Cebreiro. In this man's face, I saw the honest warmth I'd seen in many other welcoming smiles as I checked into a different *albergue* each night, foot weary, thinking of dinner and glad for a dry haven. And I thought of how I – and the others – would set off in short-lived dryness in the twilight of each dawn, praying to the heavens, in the humble hope of a sunny day ahead. And how I could never quite shake off the oh, so pervasive cold, a cold now instantly tempered by the shake of a hand and a warm flood of achievement. Well, not quite achievement yet. There were still 120 kilometres to go but 660 were now behind me. The Spaniard downed his coffee and left the room, leaving me feeling somewhat shaken yet proud. Proud to be me.

When I completed the Camino for the second time in March 2018, I arrived at Santiago only to find that the Pilgrims' Office had moved since my last visit. Santiago is not a big place and it didn't take me long to find it but emotionally I was in a bit of a strange place and so it took me longer than it should have. On this particular trip, I had saved the final seventeen kilometres to complete on my last morning and, for the first time in three weeks, the sun bore down on me as I walked... in minus five degrees. At least it was dry, I thought. Cold and dry was both different and welcome. And yet, as I walked under the clear blue and rainless sky, my eyes were continually tear-filled, so much so that it blurred my vision. As I paced out my steps, I tried to rationalise what was happening, to understand just why the tears were falling at all.

Upon finally arriving at the Pilgrim Office in Santiago de Compostela, I was, to my mind, admirably managing to control my emotions as I handed over my *credencial* to the clerk for him to date stamp, sign and approve, when suddenly a truly endearing, matronly woman moved in alongside me and asked if I had walked alone. I crumpled and my eyes filled with fresh tears as I looked at her calm face and said yes. She must have seen the raw emotion in my eyes, in my face, my entire body and demeanour because, without further word, this lovely woman moved towards me with welcoming arms outstretched and, as tenderly as she could, hugged me with such genuine kindness it made my eyes well up some more. Such was the pent up emotion of spontaneous contact, of arrival, of having walked over 780 kilometres, and spending three weeks outdoors in in the worst weather conditions I could remember. The tears were due, in part to the sudden recognition of the mental anguish I had endured dealing with this for ten hours each day and, in part to the crowning release and out-pouring of the physical pain I had suffered in order to accomplish my approximate forty kilometres per day. I cried some more until I could breathe calmly. And then I thanked her.

I said yes, I was solo. I explained that I had covered about forty kilometres each day because many *albergues* were shut and stopping to rest in non-stop, gale-force wind and rain had not been an option. But, I added, I liked to walk alone. It gave me time to think. And time not to think. And she hugged me again. She told me I was home and took my backpack from me for safe-keeping while I went to the cathedral and participated in the pilgrims' mass. I had a mild and momentary panic as suddenly I felt naked without my pack. But I inhaled deeply and forced myself to relax so that I could relish the new-found lightness this woman had given me. I was home. That's what she had said. I had done it. I had journeyed inside and out and now I had arrived home. It made me think of the poem by the Vietnamese Buddhist monk, Thich Nhat Hanh[1]: *I have arrived. I am home*. I breathed a profound breath as I realised that, on this Camino occasion just as the last, I had been on and through an extraordinary journey of self-discovery. And not only had I survived but I also felt calmer, lighter, more aware and peaceful for just being me and for knowing me a little bit better.

Ping!

Almost instantaneously a distant and vague memory came to mind, arresting my thoughts, dragging me back in time to recall another place, on another journey, in another reality.

.../...

When I was thirty-three, I sat down on a rock to die.

---

[1]The Long Road Turns to Joy

I'd had enough of life and people and I couldn't face them again. Actually, I didn't want to face them again. That was the difference. I'd spent a miserable life of tears and pain, guilt and suffering, and I didn't want anymore. I'd been so sick for so long of the poison that was in me and had become me that now I was emptied and had nothing left to give. I was become numb. I had retched myself to an obscure non-existence, a vacuum of nothingness, and all that remained was the husk of a bruised body devoid of mind and thoughts and soul.

I'd walked out of the front door up into the hills behind my home. Ha, home! That was a joke. Wasn't home supposed to be a place of safety and security? Wasn't home supposed to be a protected haven to which we retreated when outside things got too tough and painful? Where had my safe home been all my life? Too late for questions now. I no longer cared.

I'd climbed up through the fir trees oblivious to the snagging undergrowth that gouged indiscriminate bloodied lines across my legs. I saw a huge rock jutting out amidst the firs and aimed for it. Perfect. Cold and grey meets cold and emotionless. I clambered up and sat down on it, not knowing, not aware even, of how cold or uncomfortable it was. I just wanted to sit and, as I sat, I willed my body to shut down, bit by gradual bit, until every last breath was squeezed out of my lungs. Time no longer existed nor did I care. My only focus, if I still had one, was to stop living, to stop breathing, to stop being. I wanted to die. And I did. I died.

I was dead.

…/…

These experiences are what **one woman walking** is all about. It doesn't start with the Camino and it doesn't end with it. But without the Camino it could never have been written.

…/…

"If you think adventure is dangerous, try routine; it is lethal."
Paulo Coelho

Chapter One: Introduction

I distinctly remember waking up on the morning of my forty-fifth birthday, sitting bolt upright in bed at home in the south of France, and immediately knowing that this was the first day of the rest of my life. Actually, and more specifically, I remember the feeling of *knowing* that this was precisely the beginning of the second half of my life.

And suddenly it was all rather exciting. Not because it was my birthday (being born on the 26th December is not a good day to celebrate a birthday when everyone has overdosed on the festivities of the 25th) but rather what was exciting was that I knew exactly what I had to devote the rest of my life to doing... or being. In a nutshell, for the first time in my life that I could recall, I distinctly knew what my goal was or had become. Out of the blue, I knew I should spend the rest of my life learning to live life with absolutely no fear.

Now, to some this may sound a little strange, a little under-whelming in terms of the types of goals that people generally tend to manifest, a little woolly even to those who prefer to have well-defined, outcome-related targets. But I can still recall as clear as day the feeling I had of knowing the extent to which I would have to push myself in order to accomplish this goal before I died. It was almost a series of premonitions that raced at top-speed through my mind in what could have been actually little more than five seconds. Perhaps premonition is a little too spooky for some; an instinctual visual display of images may be a better description. Whatever the appropriate phrase, I was left in the full knowledge that I would be strenuously tested to go beyond the limits of my hitherto average existence and most certainly outside of my comfort zone.

At this stage, I feel obliged to add some further clarity that came to me as that particular birthday unfolded and that is my basic interpretation of fear. I don't mean the kind when someone leaps out behind you and says 'boo' to make you jump; or the idea that jumping out of a plane is a good way to get over a fear of heights (the first I disregard and I'm still weighing up the possible merits of the second). I'm talking about the fears that almost everybody in the Western world seems to acquire as we get older.

Have you ever observed how many people make excuses for not doing the things they once used to do? It's not necessarily that they no longer like doing them, it's probably more likely due to an age- or life-learned comfort factor developed from doing nothing. If consciously or unconsciously you do nothing, you are not exposing yourself to any risk, right? And so for many, they stop going out and doing things *outside*. It's too cold... it's too dangerous... it's better to be safe than sorry and not go do... I could go on with a list of negatives that people recite (kind of like a new ten commandments for some) to justify staying put behind closed and double-locked doors, not trusting neighbours or friends or society, and effectively cutting themselves off from the very life-force that feeds them: nature and the natural world. I believe these fears have also escalated recently in this new world of heightened terrorism, separation and loss of meaningful communities.

I ask my sisters to forgive me here but my experience is that women, generally-speaking, become more afraid than men of life and events that are happening all around them as they get older. Men just don't live with the same fears in this male-dominated, highly structured world. Of course, they do have their own issues, worries and fears that many spend a lifetime covering up, but that's another matter.

Back to the point. When I woke up in bed on that particular 26th December, I knew that the same fate faced by millions of other women was also being presented to me as an option: to live the rest of my life getting older, more fearful and paranoid, to the extent that (to my mind) it would eventually become unbearable and simply not worth living.

I shivered as I contemplated this. I had already been to that dark and desolate place once before and I had no intentions of going back there again.

And so, the alternative was to buck the trend and do the opposite. And this thought tickled my spirit and sense of fun.

This one thought made me feel strong and in control of myself and my life. With this one thought, I was filled with a strange sense of freedom unlike any other I had felt before. A classic Mary Shelley quotation came to mind: "Beware; for I am fearless, and therefore powerful."[2]

The core premise that came to me was that I would empower myself by walking through this false and yet tangible wall of Western world fears to a peaceful existence in which I lived more harmoniously with nature and to better mutual benefit.

And so I decided to go and walk. Out there in the countryside beyond the walls of home comfort, security and safety. Away from the buildings, towns and villages, noise of people and machines, and superficially, built-up barriers designed to keep a safe distance between humans and the natural world. Furthermore, I decided to go alone, to not take a phone as a back-up and instead trust that the universe would always provide me with whatever I may need in times both good and bad. I don't say this flippantly because, when I sat down and thought about past experiences where I had been most exposed to danger, the universal forces out there had always contrived somehow to bring me back to safety, as the reader will discover soon enough.

Oh, and one last thing to mention at this point. Waking up on my forty-fifth birthday, I had somehow acquired the belief that if I could truly learn the art and skill of having absolutely no fear – just like Jesus - then I would have absolute protection from the universe, so much so that I could not be harmed in any way. That's a big thought to think and an even

---

[2] Mary Shelley, Frankenstein

bigger premise to put to the test. And, feeling that I knew how to distinguish between being downright stupid and trusting in the flow of life (karma, grace, whatever we want to call it), I started to go out and walk to test my mettle, my intentions, my beliefs and my reserves.

And, oh boy, what lessons did I start to learn.

.../...

There are as many reasons to walk the Camino de Santiago de Compostela as there are footsteps taken to accomplish its 780 kilometres from Saint-Jean-Pied-de-Port, a traditional starting point on the French side of the Pyrenees. But you don't have to start there, you can start from your own front door and do it in as many stages as you like over days, weeks, months or years, as many have done throughout the centuries of its history.

At the end of March 2018, I finished walking the Camino for the second time. **one woman walking** is not just about walking the Camino but, without the 780 kilometres of its path, this book could not have been written for it has taught me all the heights and depths, the wonders and ordeals, the lessons and achievements, and the pains and pleasures, that walking can bring. Yet while the Camino is central to this book, it is not the beginning of it. The beginning starts with walking and, more specifically, why I walk.

Why I Walk

Rudolf Steiner once said something along the lines of: if you want to know yourself, go out and explore the world and, if you want to know the world better, look within yourself. To my mind, they are both great reasons to walk.

Back in the mid-1990s, I was sitting on a jetty at a lodge in Lake Naivasha, Kenya and I was looking out at Kilimanjaro in the distance wondering whether I should spend the rest of my life in Africa or go elsewhere. After a few hours of simply staring, I suddenly, and for no particular reason, decided to leave and so got up, packed and flew back to England that same night. A bit rash some may say but one of the questions that crossed my mind at the time was, given that I was a hundred years too late to be an explorer, what was I doing there in that place where so much discovery and exploration had already been done before?

Since that time, I've come to realise that I was never destined to be an explorer or discoverer of new world places. Walking has shown me that I am in fact an explorer of my inner world, as Steiner would say, and every time I walk now there is always a notion carefully tucked away at the back of my mind that has me wondering what it is that I'm going to discover about myself today.

But redefining exploration to refer to my inner landscape then required that I also rethink my notion of freedom and thus I had to broaden it beyond the physical sense to include spiritual, emotional and mental dimensions too. I know now that whenever I go out walking a new path or climb a mountain, I will always unearth more about my true self, my inner self, so long as I continue to let myself be open to the learning. Finding a reason to walk is therefore not necessary for me. I already have five thousand reasons to walk and they all embrace learning more about me and knowing me just a little bit better.

Mindfulness, living and breathing in the present moment, is the key to self-knowledge, awareness and ultimately freedom.

Chapter Two: The Camino and Me

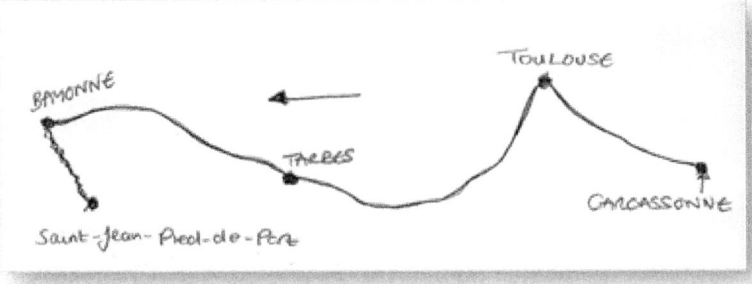

For me, it's not terribly easy to get to Saint-Jean-Pied-de-Port. Saint-Jean is a small village tucked away at the foot of the Pyrenees in the Pyrénées Atlantiques and, as such, is not well served by public transport during the winter months. I say winter months specifically because Saint-Jean-Pied-de-Port is the starting point of the famous *Camino Francés* (the French route) and so in the summer months there are literally thousands of people teeming through the streets looking for somewhere to stay the night before the big up and off on the Camino the following morning. In summer, there's plenty of transport. In winter, although I live just three hours away by car, I had to leave my home near Carcassonne at seven in the morning in order to catch my train to Toulouse, followed by a connecting train to Bayonne, and then a bus to Saint-Jean. It took all day and I arrived at seven in the evening just in time to tell the Pilgrim Office who I was, when I was intending to head up into the mountains, and to collect the traditional scallop shell to tie to my backpack to identify me as a pilgrim on the Camino.

I recalled standing at Carcassonne train station in the semi-darkness before dawn, trembling a little because of the biting wind and cold air. I was also worrying about the fact that the train had to be on time in order for me to make all my connections. But mostly, I was a bit quivery because I was starting to doubt my ability to complete the expedition I was just about to embark upon. 780 kilometres by foot over the course of three weeks: approximately forty kilometres a day. I had told everyone I would do this and now I wondered whether I could. Now it was for real and I felt a bit sick. I took a huge intake of breath and told myself to ditch my fear of the unknown immediately. Fear only ever attracts more fear.

I'd been training for two months walking between ten and forty kilometres a day in order to acclimatise my feet to the boots and the daily distances I intended to complete on the Camino. I never gave a second thought to blisters. Stamina was the issue here. My husband had recently had a hip replacement and I felt a tad guilty about swanning off to enjoy myself, doing this at a time when I thought he probably still needed a bit more help around the house. He'd insisted he'd be fine and so here I was. I rationalised that I could make it back in three weeks if I averaged forty kilometres a day and so I had upped the training. No more excuses. No more fear. I was doing this. When the train arrived, I heaved myself, my backpack and walking staff up the steps onto the train and plumped down in a seat near the baggage rack where I could watch over my portable home, the precious cargo of belongings that I needed to keep me alive and warm for the next three weeks. I was nervous and tried to ignore the nagging question that kept chomping at the bit to be heard: can I really do this? I looked out the window at the lifeless, pre-dawn landscape trying to ignore myself.

At the next station, a youngish fellow in his mid-thirties boarded, sat down opposite me and, eyeing my load, asked if I was heading out to do the Camino. Yes, I replied. He smiled and told me his mother and some friends went and did a week's walking on the Camino every year, always starting where they'd finished off the previous year. I smiled weakly wondering whether this was in fact a more sensible approach. The man asked if I was doing it alone. I said yes. He then asked how far I intended to walk each day. I replied between thirty-five and forty kilometres. He laughed and said it was impossible. Nobody did that. It was too much. I shrugged my shoulders and said I would find out.

At Toulouse I had to change train and, while I was waiting on the platform, another guy standing next to me asked whether I was heading out to Saint-Jean-Pied-de-Port. Yes, I replied. "So you're doing the Camino?" he asked and smiled at me inquisitively. I nodded. "Are you alone?" I nodded again. "How far are you thinking of going?" "All the way", I replied. "No, I meant how far each day?" I began to see a pattern emerging and, a little embarrassed now, I told him of my thirty-five to forty kilometres a day plan. "No way", came the reply and our conversation ended there.

Other People's Fear

People will tell you not to go walking on your own. Most probably they will never have been walking on their own and so have no experience of it. They will likely say it's dangerous because they have chosen to never try, preferring always to live in fear of the unknown. Don't give them any credence: believe your own inner truth, instinct and intuition. Trust your feelings and your own reason for wanting to exercise your strength and courage in order to find out who you are and all that you can be. Be mindful then of where you are, what you want and act accordingly.

At Bayonne, the sun was out and just as well. I had to sit for three hours waiting for the connecting bus to take me and a growing crowd of would-be pilgrims to Saint-Jean-Pied-de-Port. When the bus finally arrived, I got on and sat right behind the driver so I could see clearly as we made our way down the winding road before us. Listening to the people chattering around me, I learned that some were locals who had spent the day shopping in Bayonne and were now headed home to Saint-Jean after a good day out. They smiled and laughed knowingly at the number of fresh and eager pilgrims on the bus and, to let them know I understood what they were saying in French, I smiled and nodded at them. And so an inevitable discussion ensued. Why are you doing the Camino? Because I can. I like walking and I like walking a long way. Is this your first time? Yes.

Why are you doing it now in winter? Fewer people to bump into. Are you alone? Yes. How far do you intend to walk each day? About forty kilometres a day.

When the now apparently predictable retorts followed, I started to feel a little defensive. All embarrassment gone, I was shocked that every stranger I met was willing to tell me that I was setting out to achieve the impossible. Quite frankly, how could they when they didn't even know me? I sat and thought about the implications of this for a few moments. Everyone, I mean everyone, who knew me from back home would just nod and without question say of course she can do it. So why was it that everyone I didn't know was happy to tell me I couldn't? I'm not sure what that meant about the world we live in but I knew it wasn't a good sign.

I quietly dismissed the lot of them and sat staring coldly over the driver's shoulder out of the front window at the unfurling mountain road down which we were headed. The density of the trees grew as in complicit agreement with the descending twilight of dusk so that the road ahead darkened to seemingly mirror the thoughts now roiling like thunder clouds through my mind. I closed my eyes in a vain attempt to shut out the messy mass of thoughts and it was then that I had my first ping! moment of the journey. I was back in my screwed up and rebellious childhood.

…/…

When I was younger, I developed a bad habit of saying yes when others said no. Or black when they said white. It drove everyone nuts. Why did I do it, you may ask? Because I could. I couldn't help myself.

I maybe didn't start out to intentionally screw things up but it certainly turned out that way. When someone would tell me that I 'had' to do something, I would get irked and take it as a personal challenge. Nine times out of ten I would refuse and do the opposite and, downright stupidly sometimes, follow through on this whether it was good for me or not. I see now that it wasn't particularly clever and usually meant that I was the one that suffered for my stubbornness, but at the time I didn't know how else to assert myself.

Why was I always contrary and stubborn, they would say? Why was I always trying to ruin things by not going with the flow like everyone else? Why couldn't I be like my sisters and stop arguing and get on with things? My early life was continuously and audibly peppered with discontent and, while initially my natural inclination was to laugh and smile, be happy and enjoy life, at some age or another I learned to skulk on the periphery of people's grumbling moods, weighed down by their negativity towards me.

But I think they didn't understand me. Or maybe they thought that the young should just learn the ways and the wisdom of the old. I mean why else would people always want to tell me what I could or couldn't do? What I should or shouldn't be, or say or have? Were they intentionally trying to get a rise out of me? Were they just poking me to see if they could get my heckles up? Most people weren't interested in me really and so what business was my life to them anyway? Why didn't anyone ever stop and ask me what I wanted to do, think, see, feel or say? It seems so trite and so obvious now but, back then, nobody thought to ask me about me. Perhaps being individual was not an acceptable choice.

And some would wonder why I used to get angry for no apparent reason.

.../...

As I sat there gently swaying and sometimes jerking heavily in response to the movement of the bus, it reminded me that people and life jerked and swayed just the same. I inhaled deeply, trying to stay calm while same time attempting to ignore the folk around me who felt a need to try and limit me with their own limitations. Maybe they were aware of what they were doing, maybe they weren't. But there were absolutely no doubts in my mind that when people tried to prevent me from discovering my own truth (in this instance, my belief that I could achieve an average of forty kilometres a day) it was because they harboured a subconscious objection to me searching to express and explore myself because they were jealous that they couldn't bring themselves to search for their own freedom of thought, expression or action. Jealous? Perhaps not. Perhaps they were simply constrained by their fear to step out beyond their known boundaries and strive to do something a little bit different for themselves for a change. Whether it was fear or jealousy or something else, it didn't matter. Whatever it was, it was their problem not mine.

What became abundantly clear to me one day when out walking in the Pyrenees back home, happily eschewing the everyday humdrum of human busyness and materialism, was that when people tell you what you can and can't do, they are quite simply voicing their own constraints and limitations, bouncing them off you as though you are a reflective mirror. They are fearful of you when you are different because they can't place you and don't know how to act and react with you. They are both fearful and in awe of you, perhaps jealous, perhaps hateful, but almost certainly they want to stop you from being you because they are unable to be themselves. In fact, when people are downright nasty to you, they are doing no more than expressing a fear of something that resonates deeply within themselves that you are mirroring back to them and they feel a need to blame someone else for what they see, don't like and can't face. I know now that when someone is nasty to me, they are doing no more than being nasty to themselves and I shouldn't let it affect me in the slightest.

Arriving at Saint-Jean, I was once again in the right mood for the arduous Camino trek ahead and made sure to be first off the bus, claimed my backpack from the luggage hold, and started to head up the road towards the village. To my surprise, a trail of people soon started to follow me and when I turned to look questioningly without saying a word, one of them finally piped up, "We thought we should follow you because you speak French. You know what's going on." To which I just nodded a wordless okay and continued making my way up the hill. If they felt a need to speak French now, what would happen to them in Spain over the next few weeks or month, I thought. Would they be able to find their own way?

At the Auberge Municipale I quickly signed in, chose a bed and headed off into town for dinner. Unlike many, I'd saved enough money to be able to buy hot food each day of my journey. Many people can't afford to do this and buy ingredients to cook in an *albergue* each night. I was lucky, or so I considered. Much later on, when my stomach churned and struggled to keep down food each day, I didn't feel quite so lucky. But at the auberge, on the eve of most people's first day on the Camino, the mood was buoyant, as you'd expect, and adrenalin was running high. When I got back from the restaurant, people were still chattering at the kitchen tables and, while I made a cup of tea, I eavesdropped. Some people had come in groups, friends wanting to share the experience together, while others had only just met that same day or the night before. Some were relating their Camino experiences as they'd already been to Santiago and had just come back. The common language tended towards English for obvious reasons and so it was easy to pick up the underlying theme: people walked together as far as they could in order to avoid facing the kilometres ahead on their own. Interestingly, it was only those pilgrims who had walked to Santiago and also walked back (and not many do) who appeared happy to walk alone.

Self-Discovery

Many people can't motivate themselves to get out the front door unless they have someone else to walk with. It's as though they need the presence of another around them in order to *not* reconnect with nature and *not* reconnect with themselves. It's as though some people are afraid of meeting themselves and will do anything to avoid spending time alone for fear of what they may learn.

I believe that you can't beat a solo walking experience precisely because you don't see the world with the same eyes when you are half focused on another walker alongside you. When we go with someone else we don't explore our inner landscape and our outer connection with nature in the same way. We then miss things as our consciousness is compromised and, as such, we are half-emptied by the experience instead of being fully recharged and replete. Walking alone is a very powerful tool for self-discovery and not taking time out to walk alone is, to my mind, robbing ourselves of a deeper connection that could be and should be made with ourselves.

Don't get me wrong, I also like my comforts such as a shower and good meal at the end of a day's walk. I recognise I am part of the human race and welcome the company of others and sharing experiences at the end of a day on the Camino. But walking and communing with nature, reconnecting with it and myself, these can only be done through achieving a state of mindfulness that, in my early days, could only be done first and foremost by walking alone. And this is what I truly love.

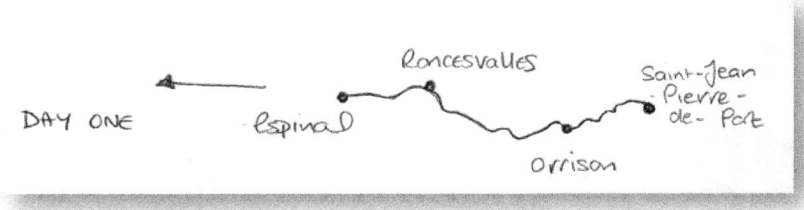

My first night was my rude introduction to sleeplessness. It's not for lack of tiredness that one doesn't sleep on the Camino; it's the never-ending, night-long snorting and snuffling, wheezing and puffing of snorers. I would later find out that even when there were only two other people in a dormitory, the Camino had inevitably turned at least one, if not both, of them into a snorer. If you don't snore, it's hell. Instead of screaming at people (which apparently isn't good Camino practise) I developed a habit of laying down for five hours, trying to still my body and calm my mind, while simultaneously willing my aching body to recover from the day's walk. If I couldn't sleep for the noise, at least I was productive and practiced mind over matter techniques until I would eventually fall into an exhausted unconsciousness at some time in the early hours of the morning. I never got more than five hours sleep a night at best. Night after night, I told myself it was just like my bivouac trips up in the mountains in summer. Except nature is not noisy after sundown, only man and his busy world carry on with their noise-making in the dark.

I guess the point of mentioning this is that it didn't help to settle the nerves when the adrenalin was already running high. Already shattered, I set off at first light the next day (and every day after that) just to make as sure as I possibly could that I would face a nice empty path ahead where I would be left to experience my own experience. As it turned out, any walker I ever met at that hour also walked alone and in silence. I presumed they walked for similar reasons to me. But on that morning, armed with a lack of sleep, edgy nerves and the negativity of strangers from the day before willing me to fail, I set off in the semi-light as bold as I could be, telling myself to be measured, not to rush, and to take one day at a time.

I got lost.

Somewhere not more than a few kilometres from Saint-Jean, I somehow managed to lose the way-markers and ended up wandering down dirt lanes in between empty fields. I cursed myself for not paying attention and for pushing on too fast. The logical part of me told me I was just frustrated and needed to be patient, calm down and work it out. The emotional side of me had tears welling up in my eyes in disbelief at my apparent failure so early on in the journey. I started to panic. If I was lost already, how on earth would I manage to get to Santiago in three weeks? I stopped to calm myself, breathe deeply and re-examine the map I'd been given at the Pilgrim Office. I felt sure I'd taken the correct route but it just didn't feel right and the layout of the lanes wasn't making sense. I heard something deep inside my head ping! and it reminded me that it wasn't the first time that I'd lost my way in life.

.../...

I don't know at what point in my life I got lost. I just remember waking up one day and I knew for sure that I had. I think it was at the same time that I lost the will to fight.

My entire life to date had been a constant battle. All I ever wanted to do was express my own true self and exist as I wanted to exist. I couldn't see anything wrong with that so long as I harmed no one else. But apparently it was not the right thing to do. Why else would everybody – I really mean pretty much everyone – be pushing me to move in the same direction as them? Why should I have to be like them, to conform and do as they did? Why did everybody want to be the same as everyone else? I really didn't get it and so, for many years, living my life was like constantly wading uphill through a never-ending mire of treacle that ever strained to suck me down under and into submission.

I didn't want to toe a line that I couldn't see, let alone believe existed. And yet, at some point I decided it was too grim. Life I mean. I didn't see the point in fighting against it anymore. And it wasn't a case of just giving in and complying with people's expectations, it was more a loss of faith in my own belief that there should be more to life and living than just putting up with the daily, tedious grind of meaninglessness. The way I saw things, people put up with lives they were really unhappy with, or worse, they absolutely hated. When I lost my faith, it wasn't that I suddenly understood why they did it, it was more that I ran out of energy to keep fighting against it.

I inherently knew that I was supposed to achieve something big one day, to be someone special, to have a purpose in life, something to be proud of and consider eminently worthy of doing. That's why I had been fighting the good fight against everyone and everything that stood in my way trying to constrain me, striving to dumb me down, attempting to suck away this precious life blood of mine that was rich in passion and hope and belief. I had faith in myself, for goodness' sake! And the penalty for this apparent crime was to be continually beaten back and trampled down – not physically – but verbally, emotionally, mentally, until eventually my spirit was crushed.

And it was. They finally did it. There came a point when my spirit faltered and I had no strength left to fight them anymore. Everyone who had ever been on my side was dead. They really were dead. I was the last one standing. And now, these others who I'd battled long and hard against becoming, they had me. I'd simply run out of strength to oppose them anymore.

With the good guys in my life all dead, I'd been left alone in my fight for freedom and for truth and I guess I ended up losing my way. Worse still, there came a point when I realised that I'd also lost my purpose, my faith, my belief in all things, but especially in myself. I didn't know who I was anymore or who and what I was meant to be.

I was lost. To myself and to life. And so I surrendered.

.../...

I must have been there breathing deeply, calming myself down, for quite some time because I didn't hear the man approach me. He asked me if I was all right. I said yes but that I was lost. Could he please tell me where I was or, better still, where the Camino was? I'd missed the trail apparently just one field back but he said it didn't matter; if I continued down the same lane the two would meet back up. I smiled and thanked the man profusely and suddenly my world was righted again.

Showing Me the Way

Whenever I go out exploring new pathways in the mountains, I inevitably get lost at some point. It always happens. That's just me getting so caught up in the delight of my surroundings that I forget to pay attention to the way-markers. When I first used to venture out walking on my own, however, I would feel irked whenever I lost my way, having missed the signs, and I'd think about how much time I would waste trying to get back on track.

Nowadays, I know better. Now when I get lost, I stay cool and I don't lose my patience. Once I know I am calm, I ask for guidance and, on more than several occasions, I have seen butterflies appear. The first time this happened, I was in no particular rush to go anywhere and, on a whim, I decided to follow them. They led me back onto the trail further on down the way. At another time, I tried the same thing again and had a similar experience. So now, if ever I'm lost and I ask for a sign, whenever I catch sight of the butterflies I don't question what's happening but simply follow them. I'm not suggesting that I get lost all the time – I don't! But the same has happened to me with buzzards and eagles where I've been searching for the next point forward and I feel my eyes drawn heaven-ward as an eagle comes into view. I know now that, if I ask in which direction I should head, it's going to show me the way.

On other occasions, I have asked out aloud to be shown a marker to point the way forward. I then calm myself and breathe deeply in and out, relaxing into the space and place of where I am. And it's quite astonishing how often, especially with my failing eyesight these days, I suddenly catch sight of a tree in the distance that seems to have a way-marker painted on it and so I head for it. And equally surprising is when, on getting there, there is no marker at all, just the patterned bark of the tree, but then a few metres further beyond I now notice a tree with a marker on it. It is in magic moments such as these that I feel as if nature is helping me, sending me the signs, encouraging me to trust to my instinct and have more faith.

Perhaps then when we venture out alone in nature it becomes natural to see beyond the physically obvious or coincidental, to see and feel more than is apparent on the surface in that moment, and to be safely steered by our nature guides. Being mindful of the signs around us, the things we normally take for granted or ignore, we are often shown the right path home.

I stood and watched the man striding away down the lane up which I'd just come as my ruffled wits began to coolly gather themselves back into some semblance of order. And while I was pulling myself together, mentally preparing for kick-off, ping!, I received another of many messages to self that I would experience while walking the Camino. When I get emotional, I don't see the real picture. I can't see the wood for the trees. When I am emotional, I need to wait until it's out of my system before a solution is going to reveal itself. What I learned to recognise then (and ever since afterwards) is that when something goes wrong, I only have to wait patiently for the right solution to turn up and it will. Someone or something turns up in my life to show me the way. I just have to be calm enough to see it so that I recognise it when it comes. Patience is the key.

Emotions

People walk for a variety of reasons: to get fresh air; a change of scenery; gentle, rhythmic exercise; to do penance (or gain relief) for some supposed wrong-doing; to climb one's own Everest; to seek solitude or a new kind of companionship; to clear the mind; or simply 'to get away from it all'. Some choose to escape their daily routine: in search of peace and quiet; to shed the daily self to relate more directly with one's inner truth; to stop and stare and see with new eyes; to indulge the senses in the open air; to be liberated from the confines of the four walls at home; to sense those moments of genuine freedom that walking can bring.

Whatever the reason, it's probably fair to say that most people are initially negatively-motivated to go out walking (I must lose weight, I need to let off some steam, I have to get away from it all, ...). We all know what it is like to be overcome by negative emotions, be upset or angry, sad or grieving. Weighed down by thoughts we can't seem to shake, often enough a change of scenery seems to be the only sensible thing to do. Whatever the original reason, most people finish by being emotionally moved by the walking experience itself and all that it brings.

When you turn to walking the great outdoors in order to find a different head space, to mull things over or seek a solution, it's interesting how the emotion starts to dissipate. It just starts to fade away, thinning out with each step, gradually disappearing to the point where you come to a blank emptiness and it's difficult to remember just how upset or angry you may have felt because the emotion simply does not exist anymore. You walk yourself into a sense of being that is firstly neutral and emotion-less but, as you continue on your way, the emotions do come back but this time they have changed and they are positive. Now you have become joyful, happy, and serene. Now your state of mind, your very state of being, is all positive.

Everyone will get to experience this if they walk for long enough. Some don't need to walk far, others do, but what is inevitable is that the negative will turn positive. Whether this phenomenon can be explained purely by the elements in soil that are nowadays also used in Prozac to help people with depression reach a happier state of being, I don't know. But what I have discovered is that often we feel consciously or subconsciously compelled to go out and walk when we need to empty ourselves of some negative emotion and, if we keep walking, whether we are aware of it or not, we are filling ourselves back up with all that is positive, peaceful and calm. From the very moment we step outside the front door and start to breathe in the living, not-stale-and-stagnant-indoor air, and feel the whisper of a breeze dancing through our hair, or hear the drizzling rain pitter-patter down on our waterproof hood, or feel the warmth of the midday sun tickling the skin on our forearms, bringing our bodies into a heightened state of sensory awareness; from this very moment, we have started our reconnection with nature and the natural world and now all healing is possible, whether it be emotional or physical. Otherwise, as sensory animals in this world, we quite simply wouldn't feel so driven to go out and do it in the first place, surely?

On one particular morning, I went out walking because I wanted to find a solution to a problem. The problem inevitably revolved around a lack of money in some form or another as it presumably does for nine tenths of the world's people. I recall going out to the woods to find space so I could think it through and find a solution. As though drawn by some invisible thread or life-force, my mind was suddenly quietened and my attention was drawn to a big and beautiful, ginger fox standing perfectly immobile next to a tree, apparently studying me.

I stand and watch him, and he stands and watches me, until after some moments he turns and walks (or I should say gracefully trots) on his way, going somewhere or going nowhere. And I find that all the things I wanted to mull over had gone, simply forgotten. I couldn't even remember what the problem was. It had become no more than a distant memory. What I did know however was that the fox had just taught me to simply sit back and watch and become my own silent, unobserved watcher. Just watch and wait, things always change. Be patient.

Ah ... Patience ... she comes to sit on my shoulder a lot ...

When emotions get a little too strong for me (usually when there are problems that I don't know how to resolve), I need to get out there and walk for a long time, not just for half an hour, but for several hours. Some people may say it's a form of evasion, a way of not dealing with things. What I find is the complete opposite. When I take time out to walk and commit myself to walking for several hours or more, I work through my emotions. I feel all the emotions I have been feeling, I fully experience them, and then walk them out of both my mind and body. And whether or not I come back with an answer to a specific problem no longer matters; but I do come back in a state of peace. I realise it's not always necessary to find solutions. The walk gives me new insight and so also puts the problem firmly back into perspective and I often don't need to do anything at all. I've worked through the emotions - so I haven't ignored them - and now I am calm. I can deal again with the next moment, the next issue, the next problem, and I haven't covered anything up.

Out walking, we walk ourselves back into a state of being, balanced with things in proper perspective, where nothing material or emotional matters. The rights and wrongs of this world no longer have any meaning because individual egos don't matter. In this state of 'balanced being' we are happy to be alive, happy to just exist in this space, in fact any space. We become fully present in the moment as we achieve utter contentment. We become free of caring and could actually be anyone, anywhere, in this serenely balanced state of mind, of body, of being.

As everyday people (or professional counsellors and psychologists) we talk of how important it is to learn to detach ourselves from worries and problems and stressful ways of living. But my experiences have shown me that when we go out walking, no conscious effort to detach is required. Rather, it's the opposite: since we do not have to think of detaching ourselves from anything, the problem detaches itself from us. Whatever it maybe, the weight of the worry or concern simply fades away, we don't have to think about it, it just goes.

And maybe that's one of the problems in society these days: we think too much; we don't just 'be' enough. Being continuously mindful of this will help us stop over-thinking and bring us back to a state of just being, enjoying the moment and loving all that we see and experience.

I followed the advice of my mysterious saviour and carried on up the lane, re-found the proper path and walked without further incident for the rest of the day. I also walked in solitude all day, trudging ever uphill through the woods or sometimes on the road when the snow was too deep. I wasn't pushing myself hard, I was just pacing. I'd practised for this and it was a pleasure. Where I lived in France there was rarely ever any snow and so walking up that silent and majestic wooded-mountain path felt magical, almost surreal, and yet I felt relaxed as in the company of old friends.

I smiled and gave myself a happy and well-deserved hug as I thought about how far I'd come down the path of self-healing since that long ago time of surrender. I knew now that I didn't have to fight for anything in life. Fighting was a misuse of energy. Nowadays, I knew that if I was fighting something it was because I'd momentarily forgotten that it was futile. What you resist persists, right? Now I know better to redirect my energy away from fighting and focus on all the constructive positives in my life, which is right where I always want to be.

I certainly wasn't lost anymore. And I didn't feel a need to fight. Instead, I was full of life and living.

Feeling Alive through Reconnection

Sitting in a building does not make you feel alive whether you are reading, watching TV or looking out of the window watching life pass you by on the outside. Whatever it is you are doing, you are not feeling alive. You are not gliding over the earth breathing in the fresh air. You are not *being* part of life. Walking outside, hearing your own breath - whether it's regular or irregular because you are walking on the flat or up a hill – reminds you that you are alive, that you have a connection with the wind dancing through the leaves, the birds singing in the trees, and that bigger place called the universe. I like to imagine that my sensory organs are sending out invisible threads of connection to weave me tighter into the unseen, etheric world. I attune my contact with the natural world, re-establishing my place in it as a fellow being of nature, feeling more at ease, comfortable and peaceful with what is in fact my natural state. The more I feel a part of it, the more I relax into it, breathe more evenly, and feel at one with myself. Sitting inside and looking out serves to remind you, consciously or unconsciously, that you are not connecting to anything natural. You are connected to energy because everything is energy and thus emits its own energy but I ask you, what sort of energy do you want to connect to? Is it part of nature or something that is unnatural? Where do you want to live? How do you want to live? Do you want to feel alive?

People often look out the window and, when they see bad weather, they decide that it's too cold or too wet for them to venture out. They are afraid to engage with elements outside of their comfort zone. Often the reasons are fear-based (fear of getting wet, fear of getting cold) and yet what they overlook (out of ignorance, laziness or misaligned comfort) is that the connection with nature is actually enhanced on these bad weather days. There's no such thing as bad weather when you are properly dressed for it and so my advice is to dress appropriately and go engage with the real world even if it's only for a ten or thirty minute walk. Your sense of exhilaration will be magnified and you'll come back cleansed and awakened by the experience. Ask anyone who does it, day in and day out. It's that reconnection that feeds us and helps us to thrive.

You are starting to connect with nature when you walk past a tree and it starts to shimmer its leaves at you and yet there is no wind. You know you are starting to connect when a bird comes to alight on a tree just in front of you, cocking its head sideways to get a better look at you and, for the next couples of minutes, he keeps hopping backward and forwarding, alighting each time on a branch slightly out of reach in front of you, just watching, taunting you, sussing you out to see if you are a part of nature too. You start to realise you are connecting when a butterfly lands on your sleeve and you know it now feels safe and has put its trust in walking in peace with you.

Walking out in nature, freedom comes to us because we allow ourselves to unfold. Sitting indoors, boxed in by four walls, we are kept enclosed focusing on whatever is at hand whether it's the TV, the computer or the phone. Allowing ourselves to walk in nature helps us to open up, become more open-minded, more creative, more willing to experience what is all around us. It helps us to see everything happening in our lives with more perspective. What you send out to the universe, you receive back. So is it any wonder that when you see beauty in every thing you walk past, when you are sending out visions of love, happiness, and wellbeing, at some point it all comes back to you too? You go home feeling a happier, more complete and satisfied person.

Each time I walk out the door there comes a point when I feel compelled to thank the universe for giving me that time, that space, that walk out there in nature. I thank the universe for the freedom, the opportunity, my health, the ability to get out there and walk and enjoy it. And I feel gratitude and, in showing gratitude, I start to bless everything I see whether it's the trees, the birds, or the landscape. I pray for healing for everything that lives in, around, over, above, and under me. I ask for healing and the wellbeing of everything because I believe that if I bless the land, the land will bless me.

And I am certain this would bring about a better engagement between humans and the natural world if we all did this.

.../...

Chapter Three: Misfit

When I was young, I played with the fairies.

When I was very, very, young, I talked to the fairies. Not just the fairies but also the unicorns, the centaurs, the bears and, in fact, any other animal magical, mystical or otherwise who came to visit and chat with me. I couldn't see these people from other realms but I knew they were there.

Without a question, I accepted they were 'real'. I believed in them and enjoyed their company. They were my friends for goodness' sake! They were my world!

When I was a young child, I was very happy to seemingly be left alone, chattering to myself. Until the point when I was told to grow up, stop fooling around in my silly world of make-believe and stop lying about people and things that didn't exist. Liar!

As a young child, the repercussions were huge. To be labelled a liar and ridiculed by parents and friends alike beckoned me towards the black hole of failure at an early age. There was something wrong with me, I was silly, no-one believed me, I wasn't good enough, everyone hated me. In my black hole, I built up an immense lack of self-belief and self-worth at an early stage in my life. I was confused and disappointed and didn't know how to behave in a grown-up world where my truth was their lie. My bedroom became my safe haven where no-one was allowed in, lest they bring their damning words along with them. I lost myself in books - other people's worlds of make-believe - as these were all the safe places to me. I dreamed of happiness and laughter and happy ever-afters.

At around eleven years old, an English teacher once said that I lacked imagination when asked to write something creative about a picture of a dowdy and sour-faced, old woman stood next to a fireplace. I wasn't inspired in the slightest, I went blank, and so I wrote nothing. I had absolutely no interest in the bland or the inane. Not only could I not identify with it but, more than that, I certainly didn't want to expose myself to more ridicule at school by sharing the potentially more entertaining stories running rife in my imagination. My imagination was for me and for me alone. It was my ultimate, safe haven.

At some point I must have made a decision to try have my parents (and others) love me and believe in me and so I ditched my make-believe friends. With it, I blanked out all my childhood memories. In one gloriously, naïve gesture of self-preservation, I embarked upon what would become a lifelong habit of: re-writing myself, starting again, opening a new chapter, re-defining myself in order to better please the people around me in my life. Every drastic event in my life brought on a need to create a fresh chapter with the latest version of me as the play unfolded and as I responded to the apparent needs and wants of others. I'm not going to go through these now otherwise the rest of the book would be meaningless. But I leave you with this thought for the time being.

The imagination is no more than a gateway to another realm. In times of (extreme) hardship, often the only way to survive is to slip into this other world. This realm then is the real world, the one that genuinely counts, because it is this one that blocks out pain and helps us survive. The implication is that if this other realm is in fact the real one, then the tangible, three-dimensional world in which everybody claims to live is false, a lie, an untruth. After all, what we believe we become and what we have in our minds is our reality. How else can we explain away all the things which are not nice in this world in which we live?

…/…

I climbed all the way to Roncesvalles through a snow-clad corridor of trees until I emerged, at last, onto an open and expansive, gloriously white-coated peak, made more magnificent as it glistened in the brilliant radiance of the sun. Until the moment I stepped out of the woods, I hadn't realised that I'd been walking in darkness all day. That in itself was a surreal moment: I'd left France in the darkness and walked into the light in Spain. After seven hours on the uphill, I was elated and glad to be over the top of the first mountain and into the Navarra region. My heart was kindled with warmth at this small measure of success after my earlier fears of failure. Not wanting to end the day just yet, I walked over to a bar, bought a beer and sat down outside on a bench alongside some skiers who were laughing and joking after a great day on the pistes. As I sat and bathed in my own happiness I shared in theirs too for a short time while I contemplated what to do next.

I hadn't thought too deeply about actual distances before setting off on the Camino. I hadn't realised, for example, that you could book beds in *albergues* in advance to ensure you had a place for the night. But then I would have felt limited if I had gone down this route. How do you know you're done until you're done, right? But Roncesvalles was different. Everyone stopped the night there. After a huge uphill from Saint-Jean, a constant climb for twenty-five kilometres, most pilgrims were shattered and so checked into the one and only *albergue municipal*. But for some reason I didn't want to. Whether it was because everyone did that and I just wanted to buck the trend or whether it was because I didn't really get a feel for the place, I don't know. I wondered what I was going to do for the remainder of the afternoon if I stayed up in that hamlet with nothing to do and this thought alone made me decide to carry on for another hour or so. And so I did. I looked at my map and saw Espinal at roughly, six flattish kilometres away. I downed my beer, donned my backpack and headed off through yet more farms and woods enjoying the serenity of the countryside and admiring the ubiquitous birds of prey.

It was getting dark by the time I reached the main road in Espinal and so I joined it and turned right, heading through the main drag of the village on my quest to find an *albergue*. It was at that point I discovered the main problem of doing the Camino in winter: fewer than a quarter of the *albergues* were open in the big towns, let alone the villages, and so I found myself in the position of trying to find just one that would be open in the middle of nowhere. I followed the signs that pointed to a few but they were all closed. I stood and breathed deeply to calm myself while I considered what to do next as the daylight waned. Rather than risk walking on for another hour to the next village, I turned and walked the opposite way out the village, off the Camino, in search of some signs of life. And I found just that. A couple of hundred metres up the road I saw a café-bar that looked pretty popular by local standards as I could see people coming and going even before I reached the doorstep.

When I got there, a woman about my age was stood in the doorway smoking a cigarette. I gave a confident *hola* and asked about a *camas para noche*. She gave me a blank look and then nodded her head towards the door. I thanked her and gratefully entered the warm building. She stepped in behind me and brusquely shouted over my head to a colleague that I needed a bed for the night before quietly slipping back outside to re-join her deserted cigarette. Her colleague waved me over and we went through the necessary paperwork to get me a bed for the night in the upstairs dormitory. Thank you!!! It was now dark outside and I was so grateful for the bed. My next new lesson of the day: don't wait until it gets dark to find a bed for the night. That could be really bad when it was sub-zero and snowing outside.

There was one other occupant in the dormitory that night, a young Danish guy who, he later confessed, had accidentally broken a tap, the consequence of which was that the hot water had run off. Instead of telling someone and getting it fixed, he let me recklessly jump into a cold shower and, realising my mistake too late, I endured my first mid-winter cold shower. It wasn't the last. Most places on the Camino gave at best tepid water and so I inevitably developed a cold that lingered on for pretty much all of three weeks. Fate or luck came to my rescue on that first evening in Spain though. I went downstairs and sat for three hours in front of a roaring fire, refusing to budge until after I was warm and toasty and I'd eaten my *menu de peregrino*, the cheap three-course meal for pilgrims. Upstairs in the unheated dormitory, the absence of others meant I could sleep with five blankets over me and listen to the rhythmic snores of the Danish guy until the early hours of the morning. Needless to say, I was ready and waiting to leave before daybreak to escape the snores in search of the peace and silence of the natural, living world outdoors.

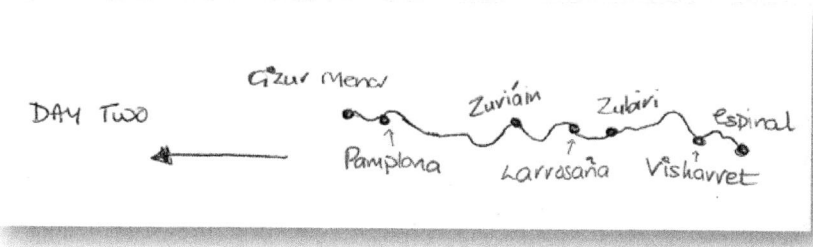

My early start was rewarded as soon as I left the village. The Camino climbed among some farming fields bordered by trees and, as I quietly padded up the snow-covered path, I had the luck to witness a fox playing by himself in the middle of an open field, merrily cavorting in the morning's fresh snowfall. I stood and watched mesmerised by the magic of the scene before me, entranced by the pure beauty and bold majesty of the fox himself. I could have stayed all day. He was clearly enjoying himself and being able to witness his playful freedom made my heart soar.

I must have done something to disturb his peace because the fox suddenly stopped and turned to look at me. Whether I made a noise or he became aware of my presence, I didn't know, but the spell was now broken. I sighed and carried on my way, elated nevertheless to have seen him at play, a thing I surely would

41

never have witnessed if I'd been mindlessly chattering with company.

The Fox

It has always been my belief that, when we are able to demonstrate an absence of fear in the natural world, we will not come under attack nor will we be threatened by anything natural because there is no reason for an animal to attack if it is not hungry. I say this with the utmost sincerity because of the wild boars and foxes I have encountered when out on my walks – we have merely exchanged looks without fear and shown no intention to harm each other.

There was a time when I set off on a big walk in a part of the Pyrenees nearest to where I lived. The trek started from a village called MontFerrier, weaved through forest up to the chateau of Montségur and from there up through more forest and open prairies to the mountain called Soularac. I called it a huge walk because the gradient was severe. I generally walk at around five kilometres per hour over gently, rolling lands but here the gradient took me down to one kilometre an hour and I literally stopped every thirty footsteps or so to catch my breath. On this particular day, as so often happens in the mountains, the weather suddenly changed and, as I re-entered the forest half way up the mountain, the fog seemed to follow me in. In fact, the fog had by now descended low enough to penetrate below the leaf line of the trees and so everything was bathed in a very surreal, green glow of some ancient, mystical world. I stopped once more, huffing and puffing, leaning heavily on my walking staff as my lungs screamed out for more of the crisp, mountain air and, in a flash, I sensed that I was being watched. I looked around me, allowing my breath to deepen, forcing my heart rate to slow down as I scanned the trees trying to identify the presence that I could now tangibly feel.

And there, absolutely stationary, statue-still among the trees some twenty metres to my left was a large red fox. He was enormous! I guessed he was out searching for food but, right now, he was just staring at me, this strange two-legged thing, huffing and puffing, hanging onto a wooden third leg to keep from falling over. I wasn't quite wheezing but he must have been a little stunned to come across this noisy, unnatural phenomenon wandering through his part of the forest. Time seemed to stand still as we both just gazed at each other, he possibly trying to work out whether I was food or a potential threat, and I just delighted to admire the raw beauty of such an animal palpably at one with his own habitat. I stood there returning the fox's gaze in a measured way, aware of my breath becoming more regular, and it felt like we both stared at each other for an eternity, seemingly accepting each other's physical presence. The thought even occurred to me that we were both enjoying the standing, the staring and studying of each other. Neither of us was afraid but when the fox had finally found his answer to my presence, he soundlessly drifted off into the undergrowth.

The day was uneventful but enjoyable as I wound my way down the mountain, in and out of the woodlands to Zubiri and onwards. I was solo on the path and so the silence of the forest was heightened and appeared to demand reverence as I passed through it. In response, I tried to lighten my step, hush my bustling backpack noise, and soon I began to feel as though I was tiptoeing my way forward with more respect in each footstep. In so doing, I was blessed to come across grazing deer from time to time who were totally undisturbed by my presence. Such moments were magical and it was events such as these that came to make my Camino such an amazing experience.

Appreciating Beauty - Being Grateful

Something that always raises my spirits, makes me smile and opens my heart in late spring and early summer is the sight and smell of the broom in full flower. And, right there in the midst of it, you'll be sure to behold the beauteous sight the bees and the butterflies dancing merrily. With the colourful sights, intoxicating scents and calming sounds

43

of these three working in harmony together, how can you not feel good about life, about yourself and all things in nature?

It occurred to me that so many of the problems with being human stem from a lack of respect for the natural world. I have discovered for myself over the years that when I'm out walking I start to develop a sense of peace as I begin to reconnect with nature. I begin to feel a strong sense of belonging and begin to see everything in a new light. It's at that point that I can appreciate the beauty of absolutely everything around me in its natural state. A dewdrop delicately poised on the edge of a cobweb thread glistening under the early morning sun is enough to warm my heart and make me smile. Dandelions, ants' nests, crows, dead leaves, mice and all manner of things I may once have considered insignificant, I now look at in a different light as I start to appreciate the beauty of them in their natural state. It's moments such as these that I constantly seek – moments that I feel grateful for - and, because I look for them, I find them, these beautiful aspects that many people take for granted or not even notice in their busy, urban, indoor lives.

Appreciating the beauty we find in nature begets gratitude and respect. In discovering a new respect for nature, nature reciprocates and reflects this respect back so that we unwittingly and yet so gracefully become more respectful of ourselves. As we open ourselves up and offer a deeper sense of love and compassion to all that we see in the natural world, we receive this love and compassion reflected back to ourselves since we too are a part of nature. In healing terms, the more we appreciate and are grateful for the beauty of everything that is of the natural world, the more we are able to appreciate and accept the beauty of ourselves.

Over time, we inevitably become calmer people demonstrating a higher sense of inner peace, tolerance and acceptance of ourselves and of others. Rather than getting angry and impatient when things go wrong, we are able to relax and laugh, accept what is and move on, flowing in sync with the natural rhythm of life as all humans should. Appreciating the beauty in all things inevitably implies gratitude and brings us to a state of grace.

When I walk for up to eight hours a day or more, my mind, body and soul shift through various phases of being, thinking and not thinking. I had already discovered this through training for the Camino and on my bivouac trips in the Corbières hills and Pyrenean mountains near where I lived. Walking in solitude on a trail meandering through the midst of a mountain forest or over a mountain ridge seemingly suspended in mid-air, is both exhilarating and immensely freeing. The more I walk, the freer I feel and, while I continually ebb and flow through periods of deep reflection and utter inner stillness, there are also times where my unfettered mind wanders aimlessly, creating both vivid and inane tales to keep me amused.

On my very first day of the Camino, as I was climbing through the snowy forest path to Roncesvalles, I noticed that an erstwhile walker had left a trail of orange peel in the middle of the path. It was hard to miss. The peel was such a vivid orange and, offset against the stark white of the snow, my first thought was: why leave it in the middle of the trail? If people want to dump stuff, they generally throw it to one side. This person had left it bang in the middle for others to walk over. Conscious or unconscious action, I wondered. As I climbed further, I saw more orange peel and so a series of questions quickly followed. The peel was fairly fresh so was the walker possibly two days ahead or less? Was the peel simply preserved by the icy snow or was it left just a few hours ago? I'd like to tell him or her not to leave it on the path. Was it a him or a her? Women would have left it to one side or hidden it, wouldn't they? More kilometres, more peel. Just how many oranges did this man eat?

Over time, I started to realise that I wasn't gaining any distance on this man. We must have the same pace, I thought. I wonder what he looks like. I'd been told I walked fast for my height and so I began to picture this man as being taller and wiry, sporting an overcoat, a large backpack and a shopping bag of oranges at the ever ready. Where did he get his supplies?

45

As the days passed, my curiosity grew in like measure and my imagination went wild. I kept following in the orange peel footsteps and the mysterious, orange man story deepened in my mind's eye.

I don't know why but I knew from the outset that I would shun the main towns and cities that I passed along the way and so, upon arriving at Pamplona, I made my way as fast as I could through and out to the other side. Pamplona is not a big city and my first impression as I approached was that it looked quite inviting set behind its walled ramparts. The moment I entered, I quickly changed my mind and made for the fastest way out, darting through the narrow lanes, chasing the yellow, arrow markers that defined the Camino trail, out to the suburbs that lay on the other side. I was shattered, my feet ached and my body was sagging with the distance already under my belt from the past two consecutive days of walking but nothing was going to change my mind. It was too busy in there! In fact, it was so busy I'd been overwhelmed. I couldn't believe the throng of people I bumped into when I entered: all that confusion, the shoving and jostling, I wasn't able to see clearly let alone think. I only knew this was alien to me right now and I needed to distance myself from it as soon as I could. And so I did, despite the pain and what would turn out to be another five kilometres on the day's walk to get to Cizur Menor. And don't get me wrong, it wasn't the people. So far on the Camino, every time I saw someone as I passed through a village or town, they always wished me a *Buen Camino*. How marvellous was that? How vastly different an experience to the strangers I'd met prior to starting the Camino who had willed me to fail. Virtually everyone I met here on the way wished me success, including the citizens of Pamplona. I just couldn't hack the volume of hustling and bustling noise.

But I must have done the right thing by limping on to Cizur Menor. As far as I could tell, there was only one *albergue* open and so I hobbled up to the grand front door and rang the bell. A woman in her mid-sixties appeared, smiling at me, waiting for me to ask the question. I gave her my best Spanish and she asked, "English?" "Yes, but I also speak French if it helps", came my reply and she looked instantly relieved. As she escorted

46

me through the maze of gardens, she explained that the Francophone quarter had more beds available that night than its Anglophone counterpart. It would appear I had just helped her out.

But more than that, this lady was an angel. She was so kind, so gentle and spoke at least five languages (in varying degrees) in her personal endeavour to assist as many pilgrims passing through as she could. Her friendliness must have been contagious (or had I just started to see things in a new light?) because wherever I looked, in the gardens or the sleeping quarters, people were being kind to each other. It wasn't the first or the last time I'd see this but people did do the nicest things for each other on the Camino. I witnessed an American girl stitch a fabric badge onto an Australian guy's pack because he has just gifted her a headscarf that she had admired. Some young girl was struggling with the constant ache in her legs and so I gave her some arnica to ease the pain. I saw a woman massaging someone's feet and patch up the blisters, perhaps one of the biggest acts of compassion of all on the Camino. Early next morning, a Camino veteran (eight times!!!) took the time to help me re-adjust my backpack because I had mentioned that it always felt wonky. I noticed one guy couldn't afford breakfast and so I left him some coins for food from the vending machines. Wherever I went, I was now searching for, and extremely happy to find, the kindness of strangers on the Camino.

Compassion

My reconnection with the natural world has heightened my observation and awareness of what is going on around me. With that, my compassion for all living things sharing the same earth space with me has deepened.

When I see an insect struggling, upturned on its back, I feel compelled to restore it to its rightful position so that it too can go on its merry way. If I see worms struggling to cross the road when the heat of the morning sun is starting to intensify, knowing they will bake before they reach the other side, I often find myself picking them up and carrying them across the road in the direction they were headed.

Once I came across a little bird sat stationary in the middle of the road, alive but perhaps stunned, I don't know, but he wasn't moving. I knew that the post van would soon be coming on its way to the next village and so I went and picked up the little fellow to carry him to the grassy verge. The bird must have known my intentions were good as he let me pick him up and take him to safety. I was about to set him down when he suddenly jumped in the palm of my hand and just as abruptly flew off. And then it struck me how brave that tiny, living being had been to allow a clumsy giant like me to pick him up. It filled my heart with joy and the tears welled as my mind grappled to fathom the deeper meaning of his trust in me.

I have placed twigs in puddles and extended branches over streams to help drenched insects clamber on else they would otherwise have surely drowned. When I can offer a lifeline of solid support it fills me with a magic sense of connectivity to be part of their world. And joy is the only way to describe my feeling when I know another living being has been saved on that day. Showing compassion is not a case of interfering with the natural processes of things, like perhaps preventing a predator from eating its prey. Compassion is about noticing when something is needlessly in pain or about to die and doing something to help save that little being, seeing it safely on its way.

In this highly demanding world in which we live today, many of us are so hard on ourselves that we don't make time for compassion. And yet, when we are able to show compassion for others, we are also showing more compassionate to ourselves. I consider it then a sign of personal evolution when we learn to give more compassion, understanding, acceptance and tolerance towards others since we are in fact also gifting these to ourselves.

When I was carving out a career in England in a society that demands over-achievement, I allowed no time for showing myself love or compassion. They were considered to be weak and thus inappropriate characteristics for serious, business people. Neither was there room for patience, tolerance or forgiveness for myself when things weren't going right or when I wasn't over-achieving. Even when no-one else was exerting pressure on me, it was amazing how much I could heap upon myself. I didn't realise at the time just how little acceptance and love I had for myself and only hindsight has shown me how damaging this was. I realise now that it wouldn't have been a sign of weakness at all. Quite the opposite, in fact. It would have demonstrated a wider, healthier and more well-balanced array of personal strengths.

Through walking, I have found the space to reflect with detachment on so many issues and to look back and see how badly I used to treat myself. I have now viewed my life from many different perspectives and these have allowed me to help heal the wounds, largely through assisting me to show myself greater compassion and love, acceptance and tolerance. As I do this, I feel myself growing as a person. I become somehow lighter and happier and freer for doing it. I am mindful of being a loving, human being in touch with the real world around me.

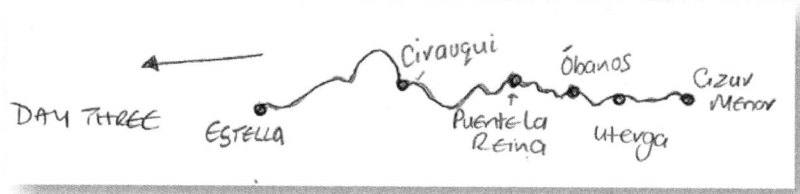

I left Cizur Menor early the next morning bearing witness to one of the most amazing sunrises I'd seen for some time and so it fuelled my already buoyant mood. It was a sharp ascent up to the monument peregrino on the Alto del Perdón but the stiff climb was rewarded with my first opportunity to gain some magnificent views of the Spanish landscape from a high vantage point. Up there, I was fed yet again, this time by that immense feeling of satisfaction and fulfilment I get whenever

I reach the top of a high peak. Looking at the vastness of the landscape spanning out around me below (which always leaves me strongly feeling my connection as a living and breathing part of it all) made me smile then and I couldn't help but think that this was what home should truly feel like.

Light Before Dawn - Reverence

It is as though time stands still while the sun rises. And yet, I am always amazed to observe how incredibly quickly the sun moves when I take the time to simply stop and watch it. As I slow down and find my stillness, time slows to a halt and the rest of the world around me also stops to revere the moment as the sun blazes, coursing along its powerful and glorious path through the sky. And I feel such reverence, such immense deep respect, because these are truly blessed and wondrous moments made for giving thanks for the sheer beauty of the land, of the earth, of the universe and for being allowed to be one small part of the experience of it all.

My mountain-top elation didn't last long. The descent down the other side was so steep it hurt my knees. I also discovered a serious problem: my boots were quite literally falling apart at the seams. The stress of the descent must have been enormous and, quite frankly, the boots weren't new: they'd already seen me through about two thousand kilometres. I was feeling devastated as I considered the implications for my Camino. Where was I going to find new boots? Could I make it all the way to Logroño in this pair? Assuming I could buy some there, how on earth could I break in new boots without getting blisters? Would I have to end my Camino early?

I walked into Puente la Reina frantically pondering the options and, to my mind, they weren't looking good. I tried to keep calm so as to remain open to new possibilities as they poured forth. To make matters worse, I found myself walking yet again in the citrus footsteps of my freshly named Orange Peel Man but now, in the midst of my dilemma, both the peel and the man were getting on my nerves.

The town clock started to strike eleven as I passed it and turned the corner. I'd barely walked past a few buildings when I saw the orange peel trail end in front of what looked like a bric-a-brac shop or small bazaar. Without pausing for breath, I entered and came face-to-face with the shop owner standing behind his small counter. He smiled and I dived right in, showing him my boot and asking whether he had glue or tape or something to fix it with. I was asking him to be my magician and he understood none of my English. But he did understand my problem and, gliding gracefully out from around his counter, he smartly walked over to a shelf and picked out a tube of leather boot glue that he proudly showed me as the perfect solution. My mind boggled. What were the chances of him having a tube of leather glue? I paid up, grabbed the glue from the counter, and virtually ran off to find a place where I could sit and have lunch, wash my boots and glue them and wait for the magic healing to happen.

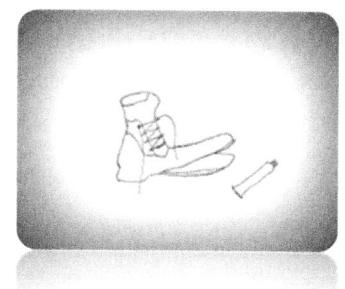

An hour later, I was in miracle heaven and off I set jubilant with the day once more. I didn't give the glue enough time to set hard to adequately withstand the next twenty kilometres but at least I now knew I could glue them and let it set over night and, if I did this every night, I wouldn't have to buy a new pair of boots. Or at least I could delay the inevitable. Perfect.

However, once again, the jubilation didn't last. By the end of the day, after walking up and down through weather blowing both hot and cold, with all the emotional fretting over my boots and the accumulating pain in my legs, I finally arrived at the small town of Estella carried along on an enormous wave of gratitude and sorely aching feet. It was early days, I was still trying to break in my Camino legs and, despite the months of training, I now realised that nothing would have prepared me for walking forty kilometres a day back-to-back, except walking forty kilometres a day back-to-back. I was so glad to reach the *albergue municipal* and settle down for the night that I was almost in tears. A bed, a shower, glued boots, food and sleep – that's all that went through my mind.

This *albergue* was busy though and I had no idea why. It was full and noisy but I didn't care. Or at least I thought I didn't. But as I lay on my bed after a lukewarm shower, allowing my legs to start their recovery process, I became aware of the voices around me, of strangers talking but, on this occasion, without any noticeable kindness. I stopped to listen and it didn't take me long to figure out what was going on. I was hearing the sounds of people grouping up. There were lengthy discussions about whose turn it was to cook or whose turn it was to wash or dry. Who should pay for this or go buy that. Complaints drifted here and there about what was unfair or unacceptable and it occurred to me that this was some bizarre, divine comedy being played out.

And yet I'd been witnessing this since the very start in Saint-Jean-Pied-de-Port. People were teaming up and forming groups in order to avoid walking alone and facing the kilometres ahead on their own. So why are they doing this, I thought? Who and what is their Camino for if it's not for themselves? Did teaming up make for a personal journey or just an experience, and were they vastly different? Were they right and was I wrong, or vice versa? I knew that I couldn't ask this question as there was no one answer. But from that moment on, I started to sidestep people, to move away from what I was witnessing and avoid being included. My Camino was for me.

Reconnecting with Nature - Rhythm and Pace

When you set off walking, if you are in a cheery mood you might well set off a little fast with a light and skippy step. If you set off sad, you may be slow and drag your heels or, if you set off angry, fast and stomping. I find there's a lot to be said for walking the earth to get the emotion out of you so that you can come back to that inner peace and joy which you unwittingly and so desperately need in your life. When you walk alone, after a certain distance, whatever pace you set off will most certainly have changed as you end up walking at your own unique pace, a pace at which you are at one with nature. When you walk with someone else, your pace is distorted as you walk at a pace that suits you both. On your own, you walk at a pace that connects you with earth and the natural world which surrounds you and of which you are a part and it is this pace which I believe helps you to heal. This natural pace puts you in rhythm with nature, of working with, seeing and hearing, smelling and tasting all there is to sense in nature and which thus helps you reconnect and blend in to become one with nature. It's at this pace that you start to feel at home with nature. This natural rhythm has a tempo that enables you to bond to the natural world with all your senses and, in so doing, generates a music that helps you to breathe, heal and renew your very sense of being.

A useful way to achieve this connection is to listen to the sound of your own breath. Even gentle walking will raise the heart rate and it is comforting to listen to the sound of the breath: the rhythmic sound of the breath comforts you and brings you back into yourself and your senses so that you now feel at home in nature. And if you wonder at what point you become aware that you have found this natural pace and your reconnection with the natural world, it's quite simple. As you move forward, gently breathing and bathing in all your senses, it's not that time stops still, it simply becomes irrelevant: it has no meaning, no purpose, it no longer exists. Your senses automatically tune you back in to your natural 'home' and you notice that when you pass the grasshoppers and crickets they continue their melodic scratching without fear of your passing. When you walk through a wood, your senses may draw you to stop and look left where you see a deer silently chewing on the verdant undergrowth and staring at you without fear. Or you turn around, compelled to look up over your shoulder and there, high in the sky, you see an eagle or buzzard watching you as you make your way onward. You are reconnecting with nature when your senses have tuned you in to heighten your awareness of your environment. Everyone and everything in your environment is aware of you and no one, no thing, is fearful.

For those who have to walk with someone else for fear of being alone, they may never actually attain that feeling of utter contentment, of pure inner happiness and connection with nature because they do not find their unique rhythmic pace. These people will probably continue to walk for health reasons but never really ever feel at ease in nature, always fearful of what's ahead or what's behind, never just walking in the moment. They may never get to attain that divine sense of inner contentment if they are not walking at their own natural rhythmic pace.

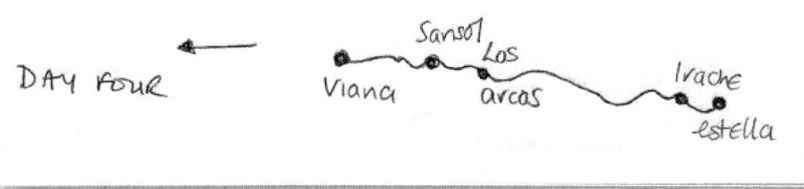

As was fast becoming my custom, early the next morning I took my belongings downstairs to pack in the kitchen. Here I disturbed no-one and could drink coffee and organise my backpack at my leisure. I was nearly always the only one to get up and off before sunrise and I loved and relished this time best for the peace and space I found on the Camino. This particular morning was cold but dry, the skies were clear and it looked as though the sun may try to surprise everyone by making a guest appearance a little later on. I walked in quiet reverence of the natural landscape, quickly falling into my own rhythm, my own pace, my own thoughts.

Not far down the road I passed the famous wine fountain at Irache where wine was freely available twenty-four hours a day to all passing pilgrims. I wondered where the undrunk wine went after I saw it disappear down the plughole and decided it wouldn't have been wasted but rather recycled. I shuddered at the thought of what could happen to it in between times and considered myself lucky to be passing so early in the day that I wasn't even remotely tempted to taste it.

The Camino was always quiet at that time of the morning and I loved to be out there already walking as the day started to wake up and get going. I was well on the way to Villamayor de Monjardín when I saw my first fellow pilgrim of the day and my eyes brimmed with tears as I watched a girl in her mid-thirties slowly advancing down the Camino on two crutches. I dried my tears and stopped to offer a friendly *hola*. I learned that she was as happy as could be to be walking the Camino and was delighted to be achieving her goal which was no more than moving forward a little at a time each day. I left her, marvelling at her courage and knowing that I had just received a reminder from the universe to think twice before I complained about my lot in life.

The descent into Los Arcos was fairly fast and I relished the prospect of lunch to buy time to consider my route ahead and figure out how far I was prepared to go. While the boot glue was holding up well, my legs and body were burning with fatigue and, weighed down by an additional ten kilos on my back, the sheer physical pain of constant, heavy-booted movement forward. I needed to recalibrate my destination and the town of Viana was looking like my new best option. The weather had taken a downturn and, while I continued to follow in the footsteps of my mystery companion, Orange Peel Man, I was looking forward to, if not the all-elusive good night's sleep then, a bed where I could at least lay flat for eight hours. My new daily Camino target was eight hours of laid out prone, very probable, un-sleeping time.

Upon arriving at Viana, I did the usual check into the *albergue*, showered and washed my clothes and, given the hour was a little earlier than usual, stepped back out into the streets to see what I could buy in the little shop I recalled breezing past on my way in. I wasn't disappointed. Vegetables and fruit (except oranges) are scarce on the

Camino in winter, especially when most shops are shut and the restaurants seemingly served only meat and chips. In this amazing little shop I bought two bananas, two bags of nuts and some dried fruit and I began to feel a little delirious with the potential health kick coming my way. I headed back to the *albergue* and sought out the kitchen for a quick coffee before I stowed my precious stash in my pack for the next day.

And it was here that I met the Spanish peace pilgrim. Sunburnt and probably looking twenty years older than he should have, he radiated health and friendliness, warmth and happiness. His English was appalling, my Spanish even worse and together we managed to get me to understand that one day he had gone out walking and, having felt absolutely filled with love, joy and happiness, he had continued to go out walking every day since. His rationale was that if he could feel love and joy while out walking, then he must also be reflecting this back wherever he went. And so this peace pilgrim was walking for love and peace and happiness for himself, humankind and the planet. Hats off to him. I thought it was a simply amazing and inspiring life adventure and wished him every continued success. I looked into the bright shining eyes of this weather-beaten man and knew he would be living a day-to-day existence on donations alone. And so, not forgetting my newly acquired Camino compassion, I offered him one of my prized bananas, a bag of nuts and five euros for the next night's bed. He was delighted and it warmed my heart to be able to help.

As the town clock chimed seven, I went and packed the remainder of my bounty and slipped back out into the rain in search of a restaurant, stopping at the first one I saw open. I was not alone. One of the tell-tale signs of a pilgrim is the hour at which he eats. Pilgrims are starving and want to eat early so they can get to bed early. The Spanish eat late. And so any queue in a restaurant at seven 'o' clock in Spain is always going to consist of a line of foreigners. I met two other pilgrims who I learned were also sleeping at the *albergue* and so did a rough headcount – four in total - I could look forward to a possible good night's sleep at last!

Over dinner, I was chatting with my fellow pilgrims and happened to mention the orange peel trail that I'd been following since the start of the Camino. I was curious to find out whether they'd had the same orange experiences as me. I was glad I didn't get time to divulge my précis of the who, what and when about my Orange Peel Man because the two of them proceeded to blow my newly, created orange peel world apart. It turned out that it wasn't a man after all; it was a woman. She was called Vicky. She'd walked with them for a few days before going on ahead alone. She loved oranges apparently. Couldn't get enough of them. Lovely lady. Bit of a fast walker too.

With each word I heard, a new image was conjured up in my head and I didn't like it one little bit. It's really hard to explain how after several days of walking the trail alone, my mind had created a whole new world that revolved around Orange Peel Man and, in fewer than five minutes, these two people had totally destroyed that version of my world, that image, my mind. Vicky was nothing like Orange Peel Man! In some respects, she was even the antithesis. Impossible! And yet here it was. My orange story was blown and my rational world was crumbling.

For anyone who has ever spent a lot of time alone (and been left perhaps a little too long with their own ruminations), you'll hear me now when I say that the effect of someone telling you white when you've been seeing black can be devastating. You have to have your wits about you and an ability to be honest with yourself in order to re-build the new truth in a whole new light because this can and does often hurt. My fantasy of Orange Peel Man was a lesson to remind me that we all create our own version of our truth, our world and what happens to us within it. It doesn't necessarily stack up that it is the only and absolute truth and we would all do well to be mindful of this.

I ate the remainder of my dinner and limped off back to the *albergue* to lay down in stunned silence on the bed and re-build my head space with an absence of oranges. My two new friends and the peace pilgrim joined me soon after and they all proceeded to snore like banshees. I was told that the Camino made snorers out of everyone but

I'm not sure I ever did. I don't think I ever slept long enough to start snoring.

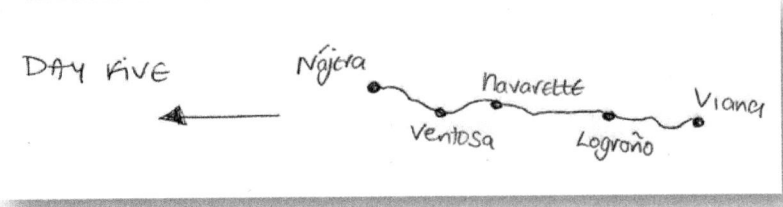

Early the next morning, I headed out into a low, black sky and the lashing rain at six 'o' clock to escape my snoring companions. At least I had a banana to look forward to en route, I thought to myself. Funny how the smallest of things can bring the greatest delight when you have nothing to worry about apart from the weather and your worldly possessions squeezed into a small pack on your back. I held out for two hours before I decided to reach round and get the banana from the pocket of my backpack. Oh my God! I'd lost the bloody thing. How the hell did that happen? My only bit of healthy, edible goodness gone! I fumed in outrage for an hour before I had the wherewithal to let it go. I knew I had to stop reflecting on how good it would have tasted if I was going to find any inner peace while out walking that day.

Being Present - Walking into the Present Moment

Doing the Camino (or any long trek lasting at least a week or more) is a wonderful opportunity to walk into the present moment because it is all that you do, day after day after day. Even if you start off each morning wondering whether you will be able to spot all the guiding, yellow Camino arrows along the way, you eventually can't help but just forget to worry, be in the moment and let your instinct take over. Your consciousness steers you towards the arrows when your mind falls silent and you open yourself up to enjoy every moment of taking one step after the other with not a care in the world. You may start off with your head full of inane chitchat (worries of the past, concerns for the future, …) but the longer you walk, as with any meditation, your head slowly begins to empty and the reverse happens as you start to spend more time in your heart rather than in your mind.

It was in walking into the present moment each day on the Camino that I came to realise that I didn't need anything in life. I realised that I didn't need possessions, I didn't need material wealth. They were irrelevant. The only thing I prayed for on a daily basis was my continued good health and the ability to walk and just be.

Henry David Thoreau argued that there was no point in going out walking if we are not fully there, being part of it, being present within it. We should be wholly there, mind, body and soul, outside living and breathing in nature, being at one with it and being healed by it. Freedom as an earthly being is found in being present, not dwelling in the past or thinking of the future, but being wholly in the here and now. Being mindful and being aware of this sets us free.

Going nowhere… I think I have always been goal-oriented and I don't know why (whether it is something I learned or was taught or just emulated from someone), but to this day part of me always wants to have a purpose, a reason for doing something. Even when I go for a walk I like to have an aim such as to reach such a point and come back or to complete a circuit doing so many kilometres or to allow my mind to empty. But there always has to be a reason….

I think what I would like to do in the future is develop the art of going nowhere, of actually learning to just go and see what happens. I don't mean for days on end without provisions, I mean just going and seeing where my feet take me, allowing my body to turn left or right guided by instinct rather than my brain. The idea of going out there walking to nowhere is appealing to me from a meditational point of view. Truly walking myself unencumbered into the present moment.

It was a straightforward walk from Viana to Logroño and, while the Camino started off meandering up and down pleasant lanes and across open fields, it inevitably led down under a blanket of grey, smoke-filled sky along an ugly, tarmacked road into the heart of an industrialised town.

Logroño is not a particularly big town but trying to follow the Camino signs through it was not easy. It could have been because of the rain, but I struggled to find the markers that sometimes appeared below your feet on the path, sometimes at the corner of a street halfway up a building, often times on their own signpost. I found myself feeling a little panicky and had to force myself to slow down and breathe deeply.

However, on the outskirts of town, as the drab and grey concrete streets began to give way to a green tree-lined path, the rain stopped and the Camino markers became more easily visible once again. I came upon a park, Parque Granjera, teeming with hundreds of water birds of all varieties and, as the sun burst through the dark, black clouds scuttling by overhead, I saw a bench and made a beeline for it, determined to go sit and watch the birds for a short while.

Chapter Four: Unloved

My mother loved water. As a child she'd won many swimming badges at school and later, after she'd married my father and had us children, we always went on holiday to the seaside where we would spend every day splashing in the waves from mid-morning until late afternoon.

As a child, my mother had no time or affection for me.

I was the middle daughter of three girls and the archetypal black sheep of the family. My relationship with my mother was tenuous at best. As a child, it would appear to me that I could never do any right. Nothing I did suited her so we were always at odds and it was only through walking that I have come to terms with this issue as well as many others. Walking has enabled me to make sense of much that has happened to me throughout my life and in cases where I haven't yet understood things that occurred I have at least developed an ability to accept them. This acceptance means I can keep growing and moving forward positively in life. And so the instance I am mentioning here, my poor relationship with my mother, obviously had a huge impact on me while I was growing up. I learned not to cry before the age of ten because it was futile and often made things worse. I can't ever recall having being hugged by my mother or hearing her say that she loved me. I felt utterly unloved and, as I rationalised things later in life, this developed into feeling unworthy of ever being loved. When I unsurprisingly became a very confused, angry and often volatile teenager, I never knew why or even where the anger had come from. I could be happy and smiling one minute and then short-tempered and angry in a flash for reasons I couldn't fathom. At the time, all I would feel was white-hot rage pumping through my veins, boiling my blood, and my body used to shake uncontrollably, my mind incapable of processing anything other than anger. Sometimes I wasn't even aware of

what was happening because the anger had
completely taken me over and, oftentimes, it
was so terribly hard to control.

…/…

I breathed deeply and admired the
grace of a pair of swans who were coyly (or
was it smugly?) drifting past a rowdy group
of squabbling ducks. And something that had been swimming deep below
the surface of my mind quite unexpectedly and abruptly went ping!

…/…

Remarkably, two memories hit me like a surreal bolt from a world
beyond.

Firstly, I recalled the day I was awarded a Joint First Class BA
Honours and, in my bubbling elation, proudly announced it to my parents
only to be rewarded with a seriously flat and understated 'Oh' that didn't
even deserve a sideways glance in my direction. Twenty-two years of wind
was instantly knocked from my sails as the TV continued to drone on in the
background. In all, it took about ten seconds to fall from the dizzying
heights of euphoria to the dark depths of a newly, found anonymity. How
embarrassing had that been? And just how stupid was I to have ever
expected any recognition anyway? There was never any room for
congratulations, encouragement or praise in my childhood and I never
announced any personal achievement ever again. I figured it would save
me much disappointment and further embarrassment in the future.

Secondly, I remembered a time in my early thirties when my
mother for some reason decided to confide in me that, because I was
apparently hyperactive as a child, she used to tie me down during the day
so that she could get some sleep. I recall a chill passing over my skin and
an inexplicable numbness setting in as I kept my eyes averted and tried to
show no outwardly signs of upset as she divulged this world-changing

scrap of news to me. It was obviously my fault that this had had to happen and so why, I wondered, was I silently choking inside?

There was no blame to be apportioned (I reasoned later on in life) but it did explain two nonsensical, recurring nightmares that I endured throughout my teenage years. In fact, they stayed with me until I left my childhood home. The one was quite simply about the thickness of rope that used to have me frequently wake up panicked and in sweats for no apparent reason. A fear of being tied up. In the other nightmare, I was terrified of being locked in a prison cell or cage knowing that I would die from claustrophobia if I was left in there too long. I used to wake up feeling confused as to why I would even be dreaming this and, in a nonsensical and answerless fervour, used to repeatedly remind myself not to do wrong or ever break the law to ensure it would never happen.

Ah... I get it now.

It would appear that at the age of maybe two or three years old, my subconscious mind (or my soul or whatever you want to call it) was already being trained to hate the indoors, love the outdoors and absolutely refuse to be tied down by anybody or anything that tried to dictate relationships which were too heavy, too restrictive or downright draining. Around the age of three, I was unwittingly being groomed to covet freedom and very possibly become a rebel to boot.

.../...

Sitting there on that bench in that moment, I saw how as a child I'd built up so many layers around me, protective layers to try and stop myself hurting, but they hadn't really worked. I couldn't remember ever being hugged by my mother (or my father for that matter). Was it because I had conveniently erased any and all memories of hugs in order to support my belief that I was an unloved child or to simply camouflage the pain of feeling unloved, or both? Love and anger. Hugs and rage.

Whenever someone used to enter into my personal space, if they upset me, I became utterly incensed. At the time it hadn't made sense but now I see how I used to retreat to my bedroom of my own volition in an attempt to find some safe place where I could be as far away as a child could possibly hope to be from the negativity that was seemingly always surrounding me and aimed at me. If negativity breached the threshold, my self-defences screamed into action because I would otherwise never have had a safe place at all. My bedroom was my safe haven, my last bastion and I had to have something to defend, surely?

As I look back now, home certainly wasn't a safe place for me as a child. It was full of painful accusations and hurtful blame, so much so that, if I wasn't locked in my room reading after school, I was out on a bike cycling round the neighbourhood until dark. When the option of university emerged, I leapt at it and applied with gusto to every university geographically situated as far away from home as possible. It was my escape plan. My get-out-of-jail card.

It's easy to reflect now but, when I was younger, that kind of reflection didn't happen because I lacked perspective. I was too immersed in the anger, the hurt and the layers that I had built up and too desperate to flee a home that didn't feel like any home my heart wanted to know. But, nowadays, I frequently find that reflection and walking go hand in hand.

One of the wonderful things about walking and making personal discoveries is the relief that comes when a sudden realisation hits home. Sometimes you get those ping! moments where something just clicks into place and you understand in one millisecond all of what happened or was going on all those years ago. And in those moments, one of several things happens: we are suddenly able to release this issue from the past and let it go instantaneously once and for all because it's now dealt with; or, we have an Eureka moment of realisation which enables us to make a sudden and often subtle shift in our thinking. This change then allows us to embark upon a new path of self-growth on which we can now develop positive habits to replace the out-dated, negative ones. Walking then can give us an instant opportunity to grow as with every foot forward we reach out to learn more about ourselves, our pasts and who we are, and thus get to know our future selves better if we so choose.

Self-Esteem

I used to drink too much and I came to realise it was my way of seeking oblivion from the things in my life that I didn't like. Rather than dealing with them, I was inadvertently tolerating them and thus subconsciously acquiescing that I was a victim of circumstance. Seeking oblivion was just a way of allowing everything to flow painlessly over me. And of course it doesn't happen like that: it hurts. A hangover hurts not just your head but your entire body. It's not good, it's not a solution and it certainly is an avoidance of the issues at heart. People I have known died from seeking oblivion in this way and it's probably why part of me deep inside knew that one day I had to stop running and face the real issues. Losing myself in alcohol, allowing the same problems to occur and recur in my life, was accepting that I wasn't good enough to deserve a solution. When I finally became aware of this, I knew at the heart of it I needed to redress first and foremost my low self-esteem.

In the West, many people suffer from low self-esteem while in the East they just don't comprehend how anyone can believe themselves to be unworthy. Whether this difference is the result of our cultural background or our immediate family (the way we are brought up) the beliefs and values we are taught at a very young age or our characters, I don't know. But I do recall a time when I was about seven years old, moving up to what was then known as middle-school, and being one of only two girls who refused to join the school choir. It took me many years to realise that already, by the age of seven, I hadn't wanted my voice to be heard. I was afraid that I wasn't good enough and was too ashamed, too embarrassed to sing. Later on in life, given that I'm not shy, I realised that I had spent a lot of time putting on a front to disguise my low self-esteem so that people would think that I was strong, I was brave, I was... what's the word... undefeatable. But in doing this, I had also denied my feminine essence, the gentle, compassionate and loving side of me, and instead lived the life of a toughened tomboy as I believed people expected from me. I deprived myself of meeting the softer side of me, allowing my feminine light to shine through, because some part of me thought that I would be revealing a key weakness, another one of the reasons behind my low self-esteem.

Low self-esteem is not just about being afraid to speak up or sing in public; it's about speaking our truth and not being worried about what other people may think or say; it's about not caring if others laugh at us, scorn or reject us. It's about being who we are. If we are not allowed by others - and do not allow ourselves - to speak our truth at an early age then obviously we are going to become blocked and confused and, as with any blockage, the energy behind it will eventually force itself out in one way or another. What child would not be confused if everything he or she did or said was wrong or unacceptable? Or that he or she should be silent and not heard in public? Or worse, invisible? I was so confused as to why I should not be allowed to be me (I couldn't understand why it was so wrong!) and my self-esteem nose-dived.

I guess one of the things about going on a long trek is that we spend time reflecting and figuring out why we are who we are and what makes us that way. If we can be honest with ourselves about what comes to light, we can often re-discover ourselves and thus have the opportunity to re-define ourselves too. Only then will we have put ourselves in a position to start dictating our own futures and that also puts us a good way down the road to finding our personal freedom too.

To discover as a grown adult that it was my child's interpretation of my disagreeably, cold and unloving relationship with my mother that had left me always feeling angry (because I never felt good enough, never right, not what she wanted) brought both relief and understanding. I could suddenly quit shaking with anger for no reason since I no longer had a reason to feel defensive about being who I was. Learning all this now, in my mid-forties, in what seemed like no more than just a few footsteps further down the trail on the Camino, one windy day in winter, meant that I could instantly stop defending myself since I now saw there was no need. I could stop wondering if I was good enough because there was no longer the question. I could stop feeling angry for no reason because the only one who had been hunting me down all this time was me.

Acceptance of how things were has come to me not only with age but largely while out walking. The distance, the perspective and the rhythmic nature of walking itself have enabled me to penetrate some of the deeper mysteries of this issue and others: walking has effectively brought me much needed therapeutic healing through acceptance, understanding and relief.

Self-Healing through Walking

I think it's fair to say that most of us develop our core issues and phobias when we are very young. I think it's equally fair to say that, by the time we are fully-fledged adults fighting our own corners out there in a seemingly adverse world, those same issues rear their heads needing to be resolved even though we will have probably forgotten why or how we acquired and developed them in the first place.

I recently heard something by Jamye Price[3] who claims one of the reasons we bite our nails is because we are fearful of the future and the world in which we live. She said we also blame ourselves, attach guilt to ourselves, for some reason and so the act of biting nails is in fact an act of self-sabotage. I was stunned when I heard this because I thought of all the things that I *didn't* do it was fear the future or the world we're living in. Especially since my forty-fifth birthday and having embarked on a quest to walk myself to a future of fearless freedom.

And then the irony hit me. If I was walking myself to a fearless future then, albeit unconsciously, that meant all my life I had been

---

[3] www.jamyeprice.com

harbouring a fear of facing the future or, more specifically, facing a world in which I felt unloved.

Now I'm not passing guilt onto parents, friends, family circumstances, anything or anyone. Perhaps I was overly sensitive as a child but I did feel unloved and misunderstood. I felt my emotional, mental and spiritual needs were not acknowledged, let alone understood, and these contributed to the development of the insecurities, phobias and fears, worries and concerns which shaped me, my outlook and my place in the world today. As a child, I was told by my mother to stop biting my nails but that was not an answer or a solution. To hear that the experiences I'd had and the way I'd felt as a child were still impacting on me today was a bit of a shock. I thought that I bit my nails because I didn't like them: they felt uncomfortable and itchy when they grew to a certain length. And then I hear that it's more likely because I don't like myself at some level, that I'm unhappy with myself, feel unworthy and unloved. It hit me to the core and something deep inside resonated so very loudly.

The next time I went for a walk I determined to think this through, to internalise it and take myself back to my childhood to see if I could pick up on anything that would help me to: firstly, stop the habit, and secondly, eradicate any subconscious fears lingering in the background. Whether I found all the reasons or not, I do not yet know. I guess only time will tell. But awareness at least gave me the opportunity to start the process of self-healing and I found that I could happily assimilate nail-biting as a physical consequence of childhood insecurity. Furthermore, I knew that now I was no longer a child living through those distressing experiences anymore, I no longer had any reason to feel insecure. There was therefore no longer any reason for this physical manifestation of internal angst to persist and so, after thirty years of trying, I found I could quite easily and instantaneously stop my nail-biting.

What I choose to do as I get up, as I walk, as I go to sleep each day, is to remind myself that I am not only loved, but I am lovable and I am loving. If I can truly accept and believe this about me each and every day, this will break the so-called, bad habit of holding on to low self-esteem. It will stop once I have stopped blaming myself, of feeling guilty and inadequate, feeling somehow that I don't fit in because I am not perfect. Well now I tell myself that I do fit in and I am perfect, just the way I am with all my perfect imperfections and, more importantly, that I have absolutely nothing to fear about being loved, being lovable and loving.

Walking enables us to reflect and find an inner quiet so that we can find answers - our own answers, no one else's - to questions we often don't even know we have and, in so doing, we are able to self-heal. Why? Because we come to the answers ourselves from within. What did Jesus say? Get up and heal thy self. The best form of healing is self-healing and I see walking as a facilitator to self-healing. It's beautiful and it's free, like all the best things in life.

I must have breathed a sigh of relief and release with this new dawning and stood up to carry on. I said my goodbyes to the water birds. Wasn't water supposed to be therapeutic and help you face up to and release your emotions? The sun was out, I felt a bit brighter within myself, and even my backpack felt strangely lighter. As I began to walk, it occurred to me that I was already carrying a pack on my back that contained everything I needed for the trip ahead. The last thing I needed to be carrying was unnecessary, extra baggage from the past. Indeed, part of this mammoth journey was about doing just that - shedding some of the weight of the past from my shoulders. Home was where the heart is and for me, right there and then, it was sat on my back containing all my worldly goods as I strolled down the Camino en route to Santiago.

Needless to say, the sensation of lightness was metaphorical, not physical, and it didn't last. Another five kilometres down the road and my body was starting to yell at me. And the message was loud and clear. After five days of walking between thirty-five and forty kilometres a day, my body was telling my head that I was done for. It was inevitable that my feet were going to swell when I was walking between eight and ten hours a day but the effect on the rest of me from such relentless impact, day after day, was such an intense pain coursing through every part of my body, I felt as though I was on fire. Every part of me screamed in agony and, even if I could have slept through the snoring at night in the *albergues*, at times the pain itself had also prevented me from falling asleep. I'd spent the past three nights laying in bed, trying not to move and willing my body to heal itself overnight. And every morning I had risen, felt energised and good enough to walk once again.

Energy-less

There are times when you might start off the day feeling absolutely shattered, exhausted, low on energy, out of sorts, or listless. And it's at these times that ninety-nine per cent of you will feel that you can't be bothered or don't have the energy to go for a walk. You may feel that you cannot muster enough energy to take even one single footstep outside the front door. And yet, it has been my experience that if you do overcome that mind-set, take that first footstep and go for a walk, no matter how short or how long, it is amazing how energised you become, how you find your body and senses are heightened as though being fed, becoming replete with nature, filling you up with as much energy as your body needs. You come back feeling better within your skin, more relaxed, more energised, in a better frame of mind, and generally in a better head space.

Each time this happens to me, I come back thinking that if I hadn't gone out for that walk my mood and general demeanour for the day would have stayed pretty much the same – listless and grey, devoid of energy and enthusiasm, leaving me in a thoroughly, undesirable place. So my message to you is that when you feel you have no energy to walk, go and do it regardless. Get out and walk a little for it feeds you precisely the right amount and sort of energy you need.

By now, the painstaking re-gluing of upper and lower sole on one of my boots had become a nightly routine. This at least appeared to be working, for now. But, on my fifth day of walking, the latest addition to my list of Camino woes was a series of red, blotchy swellings on both feet that were starting to itch. Fearing the worst, I hobbled down the Alto de San Antón into Nájera, checked into the *albergue municipal*, ceremoniously dumped my backpack on a bed and set off to find a pharmacy.

The pharmacist took one look at my feet and diagnosed the problem as being the result of excessive heat (generated through walking on tarmacked roads) staying trapped within my boots. She saw the absolute relief flood through my face, smiled sweetly as any guardian angel would, and promptly handed me a cooling, mint spray. I raced back to the *albergue*, showered and sprayed my feet and lay back on the bed to wait for the magic to happen. I finally collapsed into an exhausted sleep.

The next morning I woke with a start and went to examine my feet in the bright light of the bathroom. They were just fine, all red blotches gone. They looked normal. I thanked the heavens for small mercies, dressed and packed, and set off in the morning twilight in search of food (I was starving!), wondering why on earth I had chosen to do this in winter when finding both *albergues* and cafés open was not easy. As usual at this hour, I was alone on the path. It was cold and I knew I had to walk at least two hours (probably three) before I would find somewhere open for coffee and tortilla. I adjusted my backpack and quickly sank into the rhythmic left, right, left, right, pace I now knew so well. I think I was even sleep-walking for a part of the way.

71

The next thing I remember I stopped abruptly and hard in my tracks. I was more than wide-awake now. I had unexpectedly and quite suddenly had another one of those strange ping! moments.

.../*...*

Chapter Five: Loser

When I was fifteen I killed my grandmother.

I was about twelve years old when my grandmother came to live with us because my grandfather had suffered three strokes. A granny-flat was built on the side of our house so they could be closer to the family instead of some 200 miles away. As it turned out, my grandmother passed away before my grandfather.

When they moved in, my maternal grandmother very quickly became my protector, my surrogate mother. She was the one who hugged me and tickled me when I needed it. She was the one who bathed me the time I had my arm in a cast and couldn't help myself too well. She was the one who, when I once dropped and smashed a bottle of milk, saw tears well in my eyes as I feared the consequences and she had laughed and said, "There's no point crying over spilt milk". My grandmother became my hero; she was the one who defended me every time my mother had a go at me if something wasn't right with what I was doing or saying or how I was being. My grandmother became my greatest guardian and I suddenly began to experience this enormous sense of blissful relief. Because of her, I dared to believe that there really was a safe place called home and, while she lived with us, it really existed. It was wonderful! Someone loved me and let me live and breathe and be me!

But then, one sunny afternoon, we were watching the tennis at Wimbledon on TV and she complained of a pain in her chest. Now I had been spending my summer holiday earning pocket money by posting letters for a local business. Instead of the company paying the cost of the postage on stamps, they gave it to me, and so I had been delivering thousands of letters door-to-door on foot. But I had crippled myself bending my back instead of my knees at over a thousand letterboxes (located at the bottom of the door where I lived) and so I had been taking a course of painkillers to ease the agony. So when my grandmother said she had a pain in her chest, I rather smartly went and got one of those incredibly, effective painkillers which she obligingly took and, within two hours, she was dead.

At the delicate age of fifteen, I suddenly felt fear, such immense fear because I believed the painkiller which I'd given her had killed her. In my mid-teens, I thought it was game over. This was it, the doctors were going to find out that I had murdered my grandmother and they would inform the police and I was going to get locked up. I was absolutely terrified. I cannot express now in words the enormity of the fear I felt then. But I was so terrified of being locked up, I said nothing; not until much later anyway. But, at the time, I said nothing and nothing happened. Each day I would wake up expecting to see the police and they never came. Nothing happened. But that meant I woke up each day and, from morning to night, I lived in fear and guilt. Guilt because I had killed my grandmother, immense remorse because she was the only one who had ever defended me and had become my surrogate mother. I lived with such enormous fear and shame because I thought I had killed the very person I loved the most. To boot, I had also ruined any notion of home sweet home.

At fifteen years old, I thought the universe was sending me a timely reminder that I didn't deserve love, I wasn't good enough to be loved and so my grandmother had been removed from my life by my own sinful hands. I grieved in silence, filled with guilt and the shameful muteness of a coward, and my anger at life and living was rekindled.

…/…

I became aware that I was panting as though short of breath and forced myself to breathe deeper into my belly. In what appeared to be a millisecond, everything had been pieced together anew and I could look back and see there was no way that painkiller had killed my grandmother. Nobody told me (until many years later) that she had died of a heart attack and that, while we both sat there watching the tennis not knowing anything was amiss, she was probably already well on her way out.

I fell to my knees and broke down and cried. My body trembled with the intensity of the release and yet I didn't hold back. I couldn't hold back. I'd already held onto the pain for far too long. And now, thirty years after the event, I was finally allowing myself to grieve for the loss of my dearly, beloved grandmother. I sobbed and I heaved until there were no more tears left. It may have been an hour or more before I regained some semblance of calmness. As I knelt there spent on the damp earth, my body hurt from the intense, physical release and yet, I also felt the cool flow of relief pulsing through my blood, easing the physical pain, dissolving the mental pain, righting the wrong of not having permitted myself to grieve before.

When finally I knew I was done, I donned my backpack and was already heading down the road before it occurred to me that the pent-up guilt and anger I had carried for so many years were no more than false friends. So-called friends who had lied to me, had me believe they would protect me, when all they had really ever done was reinforce the erroneous belief that I was unworthy of being loved. More than that, I realised that I was the creator of these fake friends who used to willingly tell me that if anyone tried to love me they would most certainly be removed from my life. It was only at that moment that I could look back and see that, it was not only illogical, it simply wasn't true and a new wave of relief flowed through me. In this seeming half-sleep of a walk, I had come to a full realisation and acceptance of this entire episode in my life and I was finally liberated. I stopped and stared down the path stretching out for kilometres in front of me and I knew that I was free. I had just broken yet another link in the chain tethering me to my damaged past and, in so doing, had freed myself from yet another unnecessary burden. As I stared at the beauty of the countryside around me a smile broke out to light up my face. I had just taken a few steps further forward in my life. Deep down inside, new life was stirring and I knew I was starting to liberate myself. And it felt good.

Freedom

The more I walk, the more I come to realise that true freedom is not merely to be found in our physical sense of being. I'm also beginning to understand that true freedom is bigger than we humans can understand. After five years of searching, however, these are just a few things about freedom that I feel I am only now starting to grasp.

As an earthly being, freedom is to be found in being present, not dwelling in the past or thinking of the future, but being wholly present in each moment as it occurs. True freedom is a way of being and a state of existence.

The mere act of walking enables you, by putting one foot in front of the other, taking one step at a time, to liberate yourself from the cares and concerns of everything and everyone around you in your life. With every step you take, you become more and more one with the natural countryside in which you are walking and, the mere act of doing this puts you into that state of being free. You become freedom itself, you embody it because as you continue with your own rhythmic beat, you pace yourself into freedom. Here nothing matters, nothing can touch you, everything is just peace and beauty, love and joy.

Freedom is about being fully present in all your senses: sight, sound, touch, taste, and smell. It is these senses that help you to feel freedom in the crunch of the leaves underfoot, in the coolness of the wind on your face, in the rustle of the leaves on the trees, in the taste of the raindrops on your tongue, or in the majestic and silent flight of an eagle. And, with each sensation, you have the ability to just be, to shake off the cloak of your humanness, to exist as space or to exist as nothing in space, just being an observer and participant at the same time.

Freedom is also a sense of wellbeing. It's the ability to be utterly joyful from the inside out. It's the ability to feel grateful, lucky to be alive, and to let that feeling permeate your entire body and physical senses. It's when you feel as though you are overflowing with joy and gratitude for being alive and this sensation is bursting to get out, wanting to be heard and express itself. Indeed, when I say that I walk to find freedom, I'm walking for wellbeing and I just love feeling that sense of inner contentment that pulses and flows through me until I feel absolutely abundant.

Freedom can be found in the complete absence of fear and this necessitates the complete presence of love. I think part of being human is learning how to rid ourselves of the one and gain the other. I believe that there are only an exceptional few who are able to achieve this state with any consistency within their human experience. For the rest of us, a life of being human is about always reaching towards the one while walking further away from the other. It's a continuum and, with each step we take while out walking, we can visualise ourselves moving away from fear and moving closer towards love. Love is a reflection of the absence of fear, the fullness of being present, the awareness of moving through beauty that is always and ever constantly around us, the respect for all and every living thing.

True freedom has no room for any form of internal or external suppression. External suppression obviously refers to physical restrictions to our freedom of movement and our way of life. By internal suppression, I mean we should absolutely not subdue any of our emotions. We should allow our emotions to move through us, each and every emotion that arises, and love them and let them move on, respecting them as part of our life experience, regardless of whether popular consensus would consider them good or bad.

Freedom is about not worrying about what other people think about us and taking the time to discover who we are so that we may be able to joyfully express our own true selves to the best of our ability.

Freedom then is the absolute lack of all fear, restraints and limitations. It's the ability to be able to love completely and unreservedly, living in a state in which we feel ourselves to be truly blissful and where we are also living compassion in action.

For those of you who have tried looking for inner peace and find it hard to meditate or to empty your minds, then I suggest you try walking, and walking further than you initially had in mind. Walk with the sole aim of walking yourself into a state of peace, a state of being, a state of pure presence, where you will come to experience an absence of thinking and thus find absolute freedom. Accept also that it's not a permanent state and you have to keep coming back to find it again and again. If it was a permanent state there wouldn't be much point to having a human experience – you have to keep coming back to re-find it, reclaim it. Being present is like coming home. It is pure freedom. This is what makes the Camino and other longer treks and pilgrimages so compelling.

Walking the Camino requires days and days of trekking that help us reach the inner depths of our very being. Provided we spend some time walking alone (not hiding behind the constant companionship of fellow walkers in order to help the days pass more quickly), we will undoubtedly make some profound personal discoveries as our steps take us down the route of a personal walking meditation. I do not denigrate a thirty minute or three hour walk but what we discover about ourselves (and life and the universe) is bound to come in shorter snapshots by comparison simply because we aren't exploring our inner worlds as much as when on a longer journey. On day-long or shorter walks, there is an inevitable part of our rational mind reaching out to wonder about what we'll be having for dinner, or whether we switched the gas off, or whether we should ask the plumber around to check that leaky tap. There's always inane stuff going on in our modern day, data-filled heads. On a pilgrimage or a walk lasting a week or more away from the home environment, we finally manage to put aside the mindless, mind-filling drivel that otherwise would prevent us from achieving utter inner peace and harmony.

Every long walk I take allows me to detach completely from the nonsensical cares, worries and concerns that will carry on regardless in my absence and for which I can do nothing about anyway. A pilgrimage gives me real freedom so that I can reach deeper within the depths of my very being to learn more about who I am. Knowing me better is a way of knowing what purpose I serve on this planet and how I can help myself and others better. I have to thank the Camino de Santiago for being my first pilgrimage, for revealing to me how to achieve mindfulness, and for allowing me to experience so much more profoundly the discovery and appreciation of me.

I don't know how long I stood there but there did come a moment when I knew I was done. I remember spinning around on the spot, taking in the full 360 degree vista, and I found it so truly breath-taking that I could have stayed there for days. Instead, I smiled inwardly and proudly congratulated myself on reaching what felt like the top of a new world of possibilities.

I felt as though I was floating across the landscape as I continued my onward journey into Cirueña where I found both coffee and tortilla. As I sat alone in the café relishing my daily, staple egg and potato cake, I realised that my body was no longer hurting. I kid you not. This truly happened. It was as though I had shed the weight of yet another rock from the past from that invisible pack on my back and my body was now able to start relaxing and recover as it should have been allowed to all those years ago.

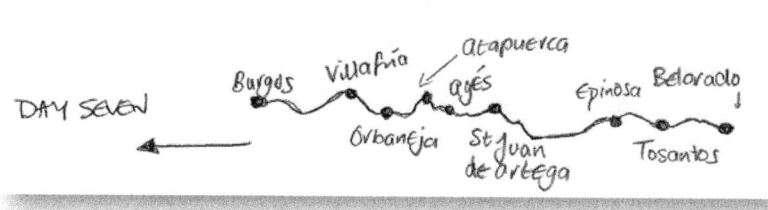

That afternoon I skipped lightly in bodily peace to Belorado and felt blessed by the fact that the rain had stopped for a while and the sun even shone intermittently as I paced out the kilometres. I slept well in the *albergue* and woke up the next morning (and every other afterwards) thanking the universe for healing my body at night so that I could get up and walk again the next day. By the following day, I was really feeling great and raring to go. There was a big twenty kilometres climb ahead of me up the Alto Pedraja and I was keen to get started. Thankfully the rain had stopped and, while the weather was cold, it was relatively benign and so off I set. I enjoyed climbing hills and mountains and so the extra uphill effort didn't bother me as it might some. However, as the morning wore on, I began to feel a little weary and wondered whether the accumulated effect of lack of sleep was taking its toll after all. Not only could the snoring be phenomenally loud, but I also faced an unfamiliar bed each night and found it difficult to adapt. I'd been getting by on about five hours sleep each night and this was a whole new ball game for me.

I managed to get to the Alto by midday and was grateful to note from the map that heading in to San Juan de Ortega would be a marginal descent. I munched on a bit of stale bread and looked at the map again. Last time I did the Camino I'd stopped at a tiny village called Cardeñuela Riopico. The only thing open had been the *albergue municipal* which normally wouldn't have been a problem. But it was huge and had no heating and I recall not having slept a wink because I'd been frozen all night. In fact, I'd lain awake with nothing else to do but wait for the sun to rise just so I could see well enough to start walking and warm myself up. This time, I'd had it in mind to avoid the place and find somewhere smaller and warmer. But the way I felt now, I didn't want to walk too far and I reckoned another thirteen kilometres would be about my limit.

I stopped for a coffee at a little café in Agés and wondered whether I shouldn't just revise my plan and stop there instead. It was funny how often some small villages seemed both open and well equipped with food and bed options and yet other larger villages had nothing to offer in winter. I came to the conclusion that I was being a bit of a wuss, thinking of comfort over walking, and determined to carry on a bit further. I asked the café owner in my best-stilted Spanish if there was an *albergue* open anywhere other than Cardeñuela. He told me that the *albergue municipal* would most certainly be open there but, if not, the *municipal* would be open in Orbaneja, just two kilometres further down the road. Brilliant, I thought. At least I had two options and so off I set.

To be fair, the weather wasn't bad. It was cold but dry as I trudged on through Atapuerca and up another Alto from where I knew from memory that I would descend pretty quickly into Cardeñuela. On arriving, I passed a double-decker bus flamboyantly painted with *albergues* and happy pilgrims parked on the outskirts of the village. I hesitated for a moment in front of a sign I saw for a private *albergue* and then, shaking my head knowing that it wouldn't be open, I carried on down the main street in search of the *albergue municipal*. So what if it's not heated, I thought, I could cope and the meal in the local café had been quite nice if I remembered rightly.

It was at that point I recalled that I should present myself at the local café in order to get access to the *albergue municipal* because the owner/manager was one and the same. So I walked on and duly turned up at the dark and definitely locked café to read the *cerrado* notice in the window that said it was closed until Easter. Fine, I thought, Orbaneja was only a further two kilometres down the road and the café owner in Agés had said this *albergue municipal* would be open in its place.

So off I set thinking of the warm shower and hot meal ahead and made good time into Orbaneja. The entire village looked closed. I wandered around and, finding nothing open, started to question where I may have missed the way-markers. I went back to the main street and this time walked out towards the other end of the village and found at last what looked to be a very appealing sight: a cosy *albergue* serving food. It smelt great! I opened the door and entered a busy room filled with presumably local custom, it being a Sunday, and the fact that everyone stopped what they were doing and turned to face me. I anxiously scanned the room, looking for the face of someone who was in charge, and I caught sight of a woman roughly the same age as me meeting my gaze dead-on. I approached her and, in my usual best Spanish, I politely asked for a bed for the night.

Over the next few minutes, I discovered that the *albergue municipal* in Orbaneja was in fact shut. Also until Easter. This place was no more than a restaurant and, no, there weren't any other *albergues* open in the village. I would have to walk on. I thanked the lady as nicely as I could through gritted teeth, knowing full well that it wasn't her fault, but I was now tired and cold and didn't relish walking on to the next village. But I had little choice and so reluctantly I turned and left and carried on down the Camino towards the next village.

Things then got worse. I discovered there was nothing open in any village. I got out the map and saw that I was in fact coming up to Burgos airport and so would have to decide whether to bypass it taking the left- or right-hand route. I chose left. I chose wrongly. I ended up having to walk yet another twelve kilometres into the heart of Burgos because everything was shut along the way. To say I was livid was an understatement. I was exhausted but pumped up with fury aimed at the café owner who had told me that one or other of the two *albergues* would be open. I felt cheated and let down. He'd lied to me. Had he done it on purpose or was he just being flippant? I couldn't believe it. Did this man know how dangerous it was to send someone off with false information when there was nothing open on the Camino in winter?

By the time I arrived at Burgos and checked into the Hotel Jacobeo, I had walked fifty kilometres that day and I was still fuming and outraged, tired and very sore of foot. I stood in a grotty shower cubicle and irritably begged the universe to give me a stronger jet of warmer water. It didn't happen.

.../...

Chapter Six: Holding On

After I finished my A levels, I went corn picking in France and met a man who would later become my fiancé. He died of a brain haemorrhage just six years later. Was it because of me that he died?

By the time I'd finished my A levels, I had become pretty nihilistic (one teacher's defining summary of me) and didn't see the point to anything. One of my English teachers came to the rescue and gave me the address of a corn farm in the south of France and said I should try it. "Just spend a few weeks of summer working and chilling down there", she had said. And so, being desperate to leave my family home at the slightest excuse, I did just that. And the freedom of being away from what for me was a place of 'never good enough' lifted my spirits instantly. I began to explore the possibility of becoming a new me that was a 'good enough' person in the eyes of all the new people I met who didn't know the old me and who didn't care either.

I met Joe the Irish boy in a bar in a back-end village near Dax and we never looked back. He lived in London and, at the end of summer, since I was going to university in London too, I moved in with him. We managed to spend a full six years of fun-packed, poverty-stricken, mostly student-style, living together before he graduated and got a proper job with BT and I ended up with a job in finance in the City. I was the happiest I had ever been. I couldn't remember a time when I had ever felt so care-free and able to enjoy life.

There was no history of brain haemorrhages in his family; or none that we knew of at the time. Joe played football each week with friends and was as fit as any other twenty-seven year old who played sport just once a week. And so, participating in a fitness day held by his employer didn't give any cause for concern. But the prolonged series of exercises over an eight-hour period apparently triggered something that had been hitherto dormant, some sort of tumour, and it leaked badly. Within a week he was dead. He had haemorrhaged so much and the hospital had been very slow to pick up on it. For the initial five days, our local doctor argued he was making it up and, by the time he understood what was going on and admitted him to a specialist brain hospital, Joe was too unstable to operate on and he subsequently died.

I remember visiting him in his hospital bed in Wimbledon on the day of his final haemorrhage and I knew at once he had decided to stop fighting for his life. He had lost his ability to speak after two days and so we had been communicating through a combination of hand gestures and eye movements. I'd spent hours trying to calm him down as I powerlessly watched the blind panic in his eyes as he fought to come back to being the person he once was. But, on this particular day, when I turned up I saw nothing but calm acceptance and peace in his eyes. Suddenly the tables were turned and I panicked and got angry and told him to keep fighting. I knew he was finally okay with the situation and he tried to comfort me but the cold reality hit me hard as I began to understand that he was leaving me. I raged and argued with him for a while, refusing to accept that he could just choose to leave in this way. He died just some hours later when I'd gone for a coffee. As I sat down in the cafeteria, something in my head exploded and I instinctively knew that something had happened to Joe. I raced back to the ward but he was gone. The doctors had taken him to the Intensive Care Unit and he never came out alive. My last words to him had been spoken in anger.

At the age of twenty-three, I was re-living the awful experience of losing the person I loved most to sudden and unequivocal death. My meltdown rationale told me that it was because I did not deserve to be loved and so it wouldn't have lasted anyway. Fate had decided so. I had just received yet another message that reinforced a reason to make me angry and to hate myself. I raged at Joe for leaving me. I seethed at the doctors and hospitals for having let this happen. I felt cheated and powerless and shook with the futility of being me. I hated myself for being *so weak and incapable of saving Joe, while at the same time feeling such immense guilt, guilt at my last angry words to him and my inability to keep him alive. I think a lot of people experience guilt when someone close dies. I felt that I should have and could have done more to prevent it, that I should have been able to stop his death or reverse events somehow. That I should not have got angry. Of course, I knew that there had been a hornet's nest of confused emotions coursing through me because history was repeating itself: the most important person in my life had been taken away from me and it was because I was not good enough, I didn't deserve love, I was unlovable. Once again, it was my fault, it was my shame.*

.../...

As I lay in my bed in the Hotel Jacobeo in Burgos desperately trying to sleep while the hotel barman insisted on speaking loudly to his customers next door, I tried to work on my patience and inner peace. Being hot-headed destroys any ability to rationalise and I knew it would only keep me awake unless I could find some inner calm. I breathed deeply in and out of my abdomen, loudly too because this always felt reassuring and comforting to me, and I lay there trying to pull together the good things that had happened on the day's walk. My angry mind was still cloaked in a shocking shade of red and so I knew I hadn't yet cooled down enough to find the happy things. So I breathed and tried not to think about the day's walk at all. Instead, I turned to the mantra Om Shanti Om and focused on finding some peace and calm from deep within me. Love. Peace. Freedom. I knew these things were right. Not anger. Not negative. Love. Peace. Freedom.

.../...

Within two days of Joe's passing, his body was flown back to Northern Ireland for the funeral at the insistence of his mother. The relationship he had enjoyed with his mother was so special, full of love and caring, protection and trust, well-meaning and respect. It would have been a mightily, cruel blow to refuse this one for her. Devoutly Catholic all her life, there was no question that she needed to have Joe's body brought

85

safely back home to be buried in the graveyard of her local church. It hurts every parent to see their child leave this world early and, where there appear to be no rational answers as to why, many turn to God for an explanation. She was no exception but, such was her deep conviction in the absolute might of God and her strength of faith in His Catholic church here on earth, she'd already accepted Joe's death as some sort of religious test and was strangely, quietly willing to give Joe over to Him, just so long as she could bury his body.

A proper Catholic burial in his home town was therefore the only fitting way to say goodbye to Joe and entrust him to God's kingdom. Accepting how religious the whole family was, and being in no emotional state to formulate my own opinion let alone voice one, I didn't argue and so flew to Belfast to say my own goodbyes to Joe over there. The next five days were surreal, intensely distressing and, at the same time, life changing to say the least. It wasn't my first trip over to Northern Ireland or to spend time with his family. But it was my first experience of religious hatred aimed directly at me.

I somehow floated through three days of funeral wake distanced from reality, cocooned by incomprehension and uncaringness about what was going on around me, wearing them as though they were some sort of self-preservation suit. I don't think anyone really noticed or cared since we were all of us reeling in our own shock. The old folk would gather around Joe's coffin at the house drinking tea and talking about inane things as they supposedly gave homage to the boy who'd left home some years ago and whom they no longer really knew. The younger ones would wait until it was an almost acceptable hour before we caved in and silently trawled off to the pub to drink away all meaningful thoughts and painful feelings because the only route we knew to finding salvation was through oblivion.

And, by the way, it wasn't safe to drink in any old pub. We were only safe in the Catholic pubs. Given that I was English and so my accent, upbringing and mannerisms were all different, it would apparently be more difficult for the locals to figure out that I wasn't Catholic and so it was decided that I should be relatively safe if I kept a low profile and didn't speak to anyone I didn't already know. For the record, I didn't consider myself to be Protestant but apparently, by default, I was and so I needed to lay low.

But the date and time of the funeral surely arrived and, blessings to my family, my father and elder sister flew in to offer their condolences and moral support. It was cold and it rained endlessly. From the time they flew in until the time they flew out later that same day, the heavens spewed forth their driving winds and cleansing rains, but it was futile. Man would have his own spoiling way and he did just that.

The funeral was dreadful.

The priest started off his elegy quite calmly but someone must have tipped him off that there were Protestants in his midst and, as soon as his condemning eyes had found me, he could no longer bring himself to show even a modicum of restraint. He was absolutely livid that there were infidels sat in his church and he blew a fuse. He couldn't contain himself out of respect for the dead or the living and he proceeded to unleash his poison through a vehement sermon that spoke nothing of Joe, the blessed person he was and the good life he had led. That priest didn't give a damn about a boy who'd just died and whose family and friends were in need of consoling. That God-damned priest used both the time and the place to lambast the forlorn hope that were the Protestants.

And inside me, the fires of my latent anger were kindled anew.

As I sat and scowled at the priest, he in turn glared daggers at me, wanting to burn his hatred on my forehead as he ranted about the abhorrently, pitiful lives of the God-less and spat out his revulsion for the mass evil that were the Protestants. My anger grew and the flames burned as though he had taken a blowtorch to my soul. It didn't matter whether I thought I was Protestant or not. I didn't care. What I did care about through my hitherto funeral-fogged haze were the feelings of all those people present who loved Joe and who were being denied their way of saying goodbye to him as they had wanted. All because of the hatred emanating from this one deluded man who believed he was speaking on behalf of his God.

I don't know why I sat there, fuming and yet voiceless, listening to that insane priest as he hissed and spat his venom, making abundantly clear to all his own personal mission of spreading hate among men on earth. Was it the coward in me that just glared and said nothing? Did I hold my peace out of respect for Joe's mother since this vile creature was also her priest? Did I stay mute for Joe's sake because I knew full well that he would have just sat there, grinning from ear to ear, knowing better than to get involved and that, in the end, it didn't matter anyway?

Perhaps I'll never know. But I seethed and I vowed that I would never trust another priest or representative of a man-made church again. I had now seen first-hand how God's chosen men could spread hatred so whole-heartedly and so vilely and it both sickened me and chilled me to the bone. I inherently knew that this priest wasn't the only one out there spreading his own poison because he was in a position of power and knew he could. But I had seen through the hypocrisy and I now knew these community leaders - purportedly cherry-picked by the divine powers that be - were no more than snivelling frauds. Mere mortals who, in my eyes, were despicable for claiming to be so much greater than the rest of us when they were, in fact, most evidently not.

In a vain attempt to blame someone for Joe's death and to ensure that the blame was firmly placed on someone other than myself, I had just tarred the Church, all religion and all priests, with my one and the same accusing brush.

…/…

I must have finally fallen asleep around two 'o' clock in the morning and, when I awoke around eight, I knew that my feet and body were grateful for the rest even though my tired eyes and sleepy head were clamouring for more. At one level, I was aware that I was still shattered from the previous day's mega hike of fifty kilometres and I was also now deeply convinced that I wasn't supposed to sleep on the Camino.

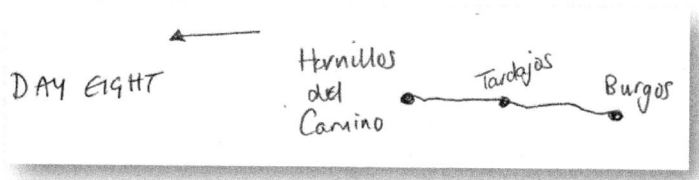

DAY EIGHT   Hornillos del Camino   Tardajos   Burgos

After the rare stay in bed until eight, I finally got up to ponder my strategy for the day ahead over breakfast in the hotel dining room. I was still groggy from the lack of sleep and the extreme distance padded out the day before but, I realised, I was also feeling quite ill. A chilling cold had finally set in and to say I was feeling under the weather was a bit of an under-statement.

Unsurprisingly, the rowdy barflies of the previous evening were not present for breakfast and so I was left in splendid isolation to wander round the room collecting all the bananas from each of the carefully prepared tables. Ha! That'd teach them for keeping me up all night! I also stuffed a few individually, wrapped cakes into my bag for good measure in case I lost all the bananas. I then settled into drinking copious amounts of coffee to try and shake off the bodily chill I'd woken up with. As I sat in my chair, slowly slurping away, my eyes wept and same time burned and I knew that, despite my newly acquired stash of bananas, I wasn't feeling very clever at all.

I finally stumbled out of the hotel around ten 'o' clock and started the long and drawn out trek to get out of the city. My body ached, my head was burning, and my throat was on fire. This was not going to be a pleasant day, I decided. And then it started to rain.

I walked for twenty-one miserable kilometres that day and my throat burned with every single footstep. Part of me can't even recall the countryside I walked through as the drops of feverish sweat on my brow merged with the rain beating down on me from on high, as I trembled all the while, forever alternating hot and cold. And yet part of me can remember the never-ending trance-like steps carrying me forward but at an unbearably, slow rate. When I stopped for coffee and food fuel at Tardajos, I knew I was beat and needed to work out a strategy of surrender for the rest of the day. I looked at the map. I would stop at Hornillos del Camino and sleep. Just twenty-one kilometres: an unheard of and unprecedented short walking day for me.

And that's what I did. Having made the plan, the remaining kilometres in the pouring rain seemed to pass a little quicker and I arrived at the *albergue municipal* on a mission to shower off my fever and die peacefully in bed until I felt better. All the gods must have been with me on that day because the lady who ran the *albergue* arrived at the same time as me and, after having given me what appeared to be a disapproving once over, nodded at me to enter and she set me before the wood burner and promptly lit a fire. On a good day it would have felt like heaven but today I was floating in and out of hell. I stayed put for an hour out of respect for the kindness the lady had shown me but I motioned my intention to shower and she helped me up the stairs. I stashed my bag on a bed nearest to the wood-burner chimney in the dormitory, desperate for any warmth I could get. I duly went and showered and then flopped pathetically into my sleeping bag, dressed in several layers of clothes and, with another three blankets draped over me, I collapsed into a grey cloud of dreamless sleep. I slept for fourteen gloriously blessed and undisturbed hours.

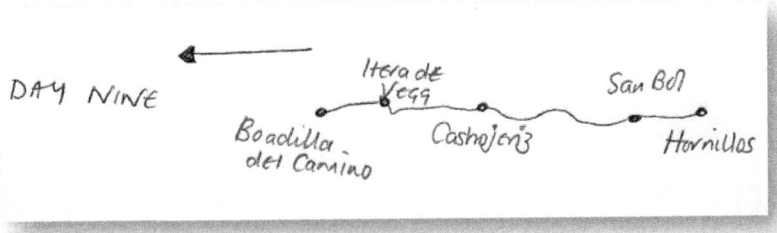

The next morning I woke up at my usual time of five-thirty and felt absolutely brilliant. I was surprised to see that the dormitory was full because I'd heard no one arrive the night before. I'd finally got some much-needed sleep and I'd been dead to the world. The past fourteen hours had also given me some incredible medicinal sleep, helping to break my fever so I was now left with not much more than a snotty nose and sore throat. I got dressed, stuffed my scant belongings into my backpack, and headed out the *albergue* door in the half-light onto the Camino once more. I was back in action and feeling relatively good.

After leaving Burgos the landscape changed drastically as I now entered the land of El Meseta, the vastest plateau I have ever traversed. The Meseta was a psychologically daunting task for many walkers because it took days and days to traverse by foot and the sheer flatness of it freaked some people out. Initially, I relished the difference and felt a surge of both peace and happiness rising in my chest as I always did when embarking on a new experience. There was hardly a hill in sight and, where eventually one was to be found, a small village had generally been built upon it. I don't think I've ever stopped so often for coffee or a snack on any other journey. But when the weather was cold and wet, or the wind and the snow had picked up again, the option of darting into a café or bar for a twenty-minute fuelling up and drying out session was always a welcome stop on this flat and barren Meseta.

By the time I arrived at the pretty town of CastroJeriz, I was looking for an excuse to stop and eat something in order to dry out once again. The constancy of the rain and the wind in the latter kilometres had started to penetrate my allegedly waterproof poncho and I wasn't excited about the prospect of getting wetter and feverish again. I made a beeline for what looked like a newly, refurbished pub, entered and ordered my staple tortilla and coffee.

A familiar face emerged from the back of the room. A Frenchman, a fellow pilgrim who started the Camino on the same day as me, came and sat down at the table next to mine, tucking back into what appeared to be a half-eaten tortilla. I smiled and we chatted and caught up on our adventures and plights of the past days since we'd left Saint-Jean. It was when Burgos came up in the conversation that I indignantly told him my story of not finding an *albergue* open in Cardeñuela or Orbaneja and having to walk fifty kilometres in one day because a café owner in Agés had lied to me.

The Frenchman stopped eating his tortilla, looked and me and said quite simply, "There was a private *albergue* open in Cardeñuela." "Impossible", I replied. The café owner told me only the *albergue municipal* would be open. The guy shook his head gently again and said, "No. The private *albergue* was definitely open because I stayed the night there. In fact, several of us stayed the night there. It was quite nice as they go." And his voice faded into the background as it dawned on me that I needn't have walked fifty kilometres into Burgos that day after all. I bit my lip, embarrassed at having ranted about the café owner, and knew this was yet another lesson: patience before anger, coolness instead of head-hot fury, understanding before judgement. Better still, no judgement at all. Just accept and let be.

The Frenchman left the café and I sat wallowing in my embarrassment wondering also whether I should stop early for the day. But, I felt as though I hadn't covered enough ground to satisfy me and I was here to walk, right? So I walked. And I got wet. And it hurt.

Being Gentle on Ourselves

I give guided walking holidays for a living and, needless to say, I meet a variety of characters while doing this. Over time, I discovered that some walkers are afraid of the forests, sometimes because of the eerie energy given off by the ancient trees, but most commonly because of the wildlife they are afraid to encounter within. On one particular occasion, a woman in her late sixties - a city-dweller all her life - was terrified when she came face-to-face with a small deer in the woods. Personally speaking, of all the creatures one could possibly hope to meet in the forest, I would have thought that a deer would rank highly because of its general reputation as being a gentle soul.

In some cultures, there is a premise which affirms that, when we are outdoors in nature and we find our awareness suddenly engaged by something such as a bird, animal or tree, for example, then nature is trying to communicate with us and has intentionally sent that thing to hold our attention in order to deliver a specific message. For many of these cultures, deer symbolises gentleness and thus seeing a deer is said to be a reminder to bring the aspect of gentle tenderness into our daily lives. I'm sure that, on this occasion, the deer was sent precisely for this reason.

We were sat on a patch of grass in a clearing quietly nibbling our sandwiches when a small deer emerged from the dense undergrowth just five metres away from us. It was about to carry on its way when it suddenly became aware of our presence and stopped dead in its tracks. We sat still and watched it. It turned to study us, presumably trying to determine if we presented some sort of threat. I was happy to simply sit and admire the beauty of this small creature for as long as it would stay. Just seeing it stood so close to us made me smile. But my companion was frightened by the deer's presence and proximity and I could tangibly feel her fear escalating as she stared hard at the small deer, transfixed and frozen to the spot.

At first, the deer did nothing other than stare right back at her. However, as it did, the woman's terror grew and I could sense the panic emanating from her. Needless to say, the deer similarly started to become visibly agitated. From an initial starting point of being gentle, peaceful and mildly curious, the deer soon became distressed and began to defiantly stomp one of its fore legs, to my mind a clear message to tell my companion to move on. It was evident that the deer was now extremely uncomfortable in the presence of this woman but my walking companion wasn't even aware of the impact of her own actions and reactions. Eventually, becoming ever more fearful, she finally decided her next course of action was to get up and run away, but the deer beat her to it and bolted first.

It was interesting to note, however, that it was the woman's fear that had influenced the deer, making it wary of the human's negative response and not the other way around. It was also abundantly clear to me that the deer was there to deliver a message specifically to this woman because it hadn't even acknowledged me. From the week I spent walking with her and getting to know her a little, I had surmised that she was a hard lady, tough on herself and on others, and it is my belief that this deer had shown up in her life to tell her to ease up, be gentle and show a little more loving kindness to herself and to others.

In that moment, I also understood that the qualities that attract us to certain individuals are the qualities that we often, consciously or subconsciously, like and identify with within ourselves. Reciprocally, the things we don't like in people are qualities that we ourselves also possess but we either suppress or deny them, consciously or subconsciously, in order to move further away from them. When we say we don't identify with people bearing these qualities, it is because we don't want to associate with that which we don't like about ourselves.

When that deer turned up to deliver a message to my walking companion, even though it outwardly ignored me, I realised that it was also sending me the same implicit message. I recognised that I can often be tough on myself and on others too. I also needed to ease up from time to time and show more loving kindness to myself and to others. The appearance of the deer on that day had enlightened my consciousness and helped bring my ego back into check.

It also occurred to me that many of us have developed a fear of animals because we don't understand them, don't know how to read them and thus don't know how to relate to them. As a race, we have

94

become more and more separated from everyone and everything around us and this separation is the root of all our fears. We humans have learned to fear animals, other humans, and ourselves. In fact, we fear everything so much so that we no longer know how to read and know ourselves, let alone each other. Walking helps bring us back into the world and rebuild those vital inter-connections.

Without them, we are nothing. We are lost.

It's twenty kilometres from Castrojeriz to Boadilla del Camino and it rained every single step of the way. Not just gentle, refreshing rain. Big, heavy drops were hitting me like bullets from above and, thanks to the gale-force winds, fully face-on too as I battled my way over the bare, open lands, screaming with rage at the weather for at least ten kilometres. I couldn't believe it! Here I was, out in the open, with no chance of a bus or taxi, no shelter or refuge, no option but to carry on to the next village while the rain pummelled my head and legs as I quite literally bent over double, fighting against the wind, trying not to get completely soaked. I failed. I was utterly drenched and I fumed. I was so angry that I was shaking despite the weight of the pack on my back that usually kept me anchored. I stomped ferociously onwards, kicking at stones and cursing when I slid in the muddy puddles. I got thoroughly soaked to the skin because, while my backpack was waterproof, I was not. I was freezing and yet my blood boiled as I screamed obscenities up to the skies. I kicked and I yelled, I swore at myself and I cursed God, partly because I felt exasperated at the lack of options, but mainly because I considered myself to have been cheated, dumped on, picked on, taken advantage of... I was ill for God's sake! This was just so unfair! And I raged at myself for my own weakness and the situation that I was powerless to change. And it was so obviously God's fault for sending me this cursed weather.

…/…

I was getting tired of life and the trials it was throwing my way: taking away everyone I loved and who loved me; leaving me to suffer in isolated misery; leaving me to ruminate about the hopelessness of trying so hard to be a better person, a good person; leaving me hurt more deeply each time that I failed. I still had some fight left in me though and so I turned my anger away from me and threw it at God and His damn church instead.

I have never been a religious person despite (or because of) being forced to go to Sunday school for a year. We three sisters somehow got kicked out, presumably because we showed no interest or talked too much or both. Whatever it was, I never went to church afterwards and wasn't interested in the slightest. While some part of me knew that the poor behaviour of the priest at Joe's funeral reflected nothing more than the immature and ego-centric nature of the man himself, part of me decided that this too was God's fault. Wasn't He the one who orchestrated everything? Wasn't it His fault that all the good people in my life were now dead? Taken from me so that I was left to suffer the misery of life on my own? Wasn't it God who was denying me happiness in my life?

Somehow, somewhere along the way, I decided that the fault for my miserable life had to belong to someone and it wasn't going to be me anymore. I was tired of pointing the accusing finger at me and so I turned it towards God. Since it was claimed that all life belonged to God, it was evidently His fault and I handed over full responsibility to Him. We, the people, were no more than puppets being played at His whim and I was clearly livid with what He was doing to me.

.../...

The rain had virtually stopped by the time I arrived at Boadilla del Camino. I had vented myself to a throaty exhaustion and was now more accepting of the weather, not so much with grace, but rather a mental numbness. But as also happens on a walk, it was impossible to hold onto a bad mood for very long. I was calm now and wasted no time in making a bee-line for the nearest *albergue* with an *abierto* sign in the window. Not only did I manage to get a hot shower, but a bunk bed next to a radiator that was actually switched on and emitting some heat! I thought I'd found heaven and fleetingly marvelled at God's change of heart as I carefully arranged my washed socks, t-shirt and underwear over the top of the radiator, leaving them to toast gently for the next few hours. The *albergue* host was a young and funny guy. He spoke excellent English and joked light-heartedly with the handful of guests he had that night about the weather on the Meseta. Dinner was also heaven sent. His mother had made two soups to feed the soul - one garlic and one lentil - and I greedily guzzled them (yes, both) down. Over dinner, I also found out that this place was the only *albergue* open in town and so, by the same thinking, I figured God must have pointed me to it. Thanks, God! Who knows, I grinned wryly, perhaps He's not such a bad guy after all. I didn't dwell on it. I was thankfully fed and warm and looking forward to a great night's sleep in a heated room. Not quite bliss but it wasn't far from it.

Incidentally, I can't say that I believe in one definitive God or Creator but many experiences like the one above have led me to believe in universal energies that steer and guide us, protect us and help us, even in the toughest of times. For me, the term God has been linked for too long to the man-made church and, given the latter's poor track record in humane matters, it really had no appeal for me whatsoever. After my experience of feeling so utterly let down by the priest at Joe's funeral, I didn't appreciate anyone telling me how and what I should think, especially in all things spiritual. I like to find my own way in life and make my own mistakes and I particularly want to choose my own spiritual experiences. It is my belief that our spiritual experiences are undeniably individual, intensely personal and, for these reasons alone, for each of us to discover for ourselves. No one else can give us those experiences.

The way I see things, if I am to have a church, I choose my church to be the natural world. Each step I take on the Camino (or anywhere outdoors), I consider as my way of communing with God within the realms of my church. I try to be mindful of moving through the world with grace and respect because it is sacred. Everything I see, smell, touch, hear or taste in this natural world is divine and that is why I am so moved by it. The natural world is my healing tank, my refuge, my place of safety. My religion is walking in nature: it's a divine place and space that makes me reverent and keeps me humble and sincere. It is here that I am at peace and, whenever I find inner peace, I can only be bringing greater peace to all around me too.

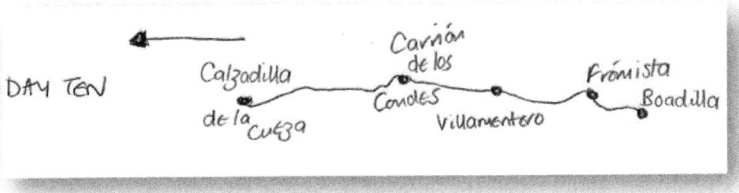

As usual, the next morning I was up and ready and raring to go, dry, fed and refreshed as I was. I made good time from Boadilla to Frómista but marched straight on through as I knew from experience that nothing would be open at this ungodly hour. Leaving Frómista and walking to Carrión de los Condes was an odd bit of the Camino to me. Suddenly bollards bearing the Camino scallop shell appeared, not just one at a time but four at a time, and at regular intervals which didn't make sense to me. Here was a virtually straight part of the path that stretched out visibly for kilometres ahead and it had way-markers dotted all the way along it. And yet, in the towns and cities where it was often difficult to spot the markers at all, there were infinitely fewer. Were they here then just to fill up some of the open Meseta or to keep the pilgrim mind entertained with banal thought? My mind boggled.

After nineteen kilometres, I stopped at Carrión for a coffee and to get out of the rain and dry out a little. I looked at the map and saw that Terradillos de los Templarios was another twenty-seven kilometres away. I was pretty sure that it was a push too far but, downing the dregs of my coffee, I buttoned up my coat, donned my pack and set out regardless on what, to my mind, was the freakiest stretch of the Camino yet. I effectively had to walk another seventeen kilometres before I saw any signs of life at all. There was, quite literally, nothing. This part of the Camino was also the Via Aquitana, the old Roman road, that traversed the Meseta and it was desolate. There were no leaves on the trees, no buildings, no birds. I was surrounded by field upon field for as far as I could see and which, at that time of year, were empty and barren and added to convey the surreal atmosphere of an abandoned place.

As I set out to walk on this particular mid-March afternoon, the sun had now determined he would come out with all the force he could possibly muster. As I paced out my steps along the Via Aquitana, I had the strangest sensation that I was walking forward and yet getting nowhere. I tried to busy my mind and the first image that came to me was of Dorothy and The Wizard of Oz. That was it! I felt precisely like Dorothy as she must have when she ambled down her endless, yellow, brick road. Except she had had company and I had none. I looked at the Camino spanning out before me and turned it yellow in my mind's eye. 'Follow the yellow, brick road. Follow the yellow, brick road. Follow, follow, follow, follow, follow the yellow, brick road'. I attempted to skip but soon gave it up; my backpack was far too cumbersome for that sort of trick. So I walked and I walked and I walked, singing to my inner Dorothy until my voice dried up in the heat of the trail.

As the sun rose higher, I got hotter, and the weight of my backpack appeared to get heavier as well. It was while I was trudging along, step after weary step, sensing the sun's rays burning my left ear, that I began to imagine that I was lost in a vast desert, moving forward, going somewhere, yet getting nowhere. I felt a little panicky and started to wonder if I had somehow managed to go the wrong way after all. But how could I, I reasoned, when there was absolutely nothing in sight but this path? I stopped to try a magic Dorothy trick and, with my eyes squeezed tightly shut, clicked my heels together and affirmed: 'There's no place like home. There's no place like home. There's no place like home.' It was then that I had another ping! moment.

...\...

Chapter Seven: Running Away

In the midst of my emotional meltdown, I ran away. To Africa.

Not long after Joe's death, I emotionally shut down. I mentally and physically couldn't cope anymore and so I switched my emotions off and went cold instead. In hindsight, I should have had some seriously good counselling but, in those days, it wasn't an option. As far as I knew, grieving and dealing with death were things you figured out for yourself.

Throughout this time, both Joe's family and my mother had begun to harangue me incessantly with their best advice on how to deal with life and death and everything in between. Joe's family wanted a share in my flat and my mother wanted to start mothering me for the first time in my life. It was too late for the latter (I certainly wasn't going to start being mothered now) and I was downright sure the first wasn't going to happen either. I'm sure they meant well but their inability to come even close to understanding what I was going through, coupled with trying to tell me what I should and shouldn't next do with my life, meant that I was now living a new kind of nightmare. I'd hardened myself up over the years learning to self-survive and be street aware and I wasn't going to give up my independence without a fight. Or perhaps I was.

My head in an absolute mess, I engaged in some serious drinking to drown away my sorrows and, most importantly, to deaden the pain. Somehow numbness made everything bearable and so, in my vain attempt to not think or feel, my new life goal was numbness. In the midst of this drunken haze, I was working in the City when an opportunity came from my boss to go work in Zambia. He told me that his father had died and the accountant had been milking a lot of the money out of the business. They needed someone to sort it out. A glimmer of light lit up at the back of my alcohol-fugged brain as I saw a chance to go somewhere I'd never even heard of at that age: Zambia. How brilliant was that? Go and help stop the fraud, get the business back on an even keel, and the perfect opportunity to run away to boot. Africa: the perfect place to run to. Lost out there, I could escape from another ruined home, from life, from me. Zambia: the perfect place to lose myself or reinvent myself yet again, if I so chose.

And so, run away, that's precisely what I did. I took the coward's route out and I ran.

I flew to Lusaka and then onwards to Mufulira in the Copperbelt region, home to the (then) largest underground copper mine in the world. I spent two years sorting out the company before realising that I'd outgrown both the village and the business. I applied for a job at the Finnish Embassy in Lusaka and, for a while, immersed myself in managing their road and forestry projects and having fun writing economic reports for the monthly EU meetings (my first degree was in Economics). I bored easily though and so moved into a marketing role at the Zambia National Commercial Bank and became the first white woman to join the group. I wasn't popular and, when the CEO was removed for fraud, all my protection was removed too. The deputy CEO had me booted out within hours afterwards. Left with nothing else to do, I embarked on a period of writing bid reports for companies seeking funds for expansion projects and this took me from Zambia to South Africa and Kenya.

I guess the point of mentioning this is that for the next five years my home was a large suitcase. I travelled backwards and forwards across Africa, always alone, and this exposed me to a certain amount of danger. Please bear with me through the following incidents I describe in the hope of better illustrating this point.

In Lusaka, leaving a supermarket one night, I saw two guys shot dead as they were breaking into the car next to mine. No warning, no words, no nothing. Just killing. Another time, I was leaving the same place when a crowd of local boys moved in on me, presumably to steal my bags, when someone kindly stepped in, grabbed a bottle from one of my bags, smashed it against a wall and started to brandish it at the boys while screaming obscenities at the same time. They melted back into the shadows quickly and quietly and I thanked my saviour.

I remember working on a farm in the back end of nowhere and, coming back from a walk one day, found a cobra coiled on the doorstep. I thought myself clever for putting on my sunglasses so it couldn't blind me and walked closer to inspect this novelty. The security guard pelted it with stones until it slithered away and it was only then I naively realised it could have bitten me anyway, with or without the sunglasses.

The power frequently went down in Africa and so businesses that could afford generators had them. While working in a lodge in Naivasha one time, the electricity went off after sundown and so I decided to leave my hut and head up to the main lodge for some light and food. It was already pitch black outside and so the only light there was came from the moon and the main lodge. Gingerly, I moved forward across the blacked-out land, drawn by the light of the lodge which I was also using to guide my feet. As I inched my way forward, I saw the outline of a bush in front of me suddenly move. I halted and blinked, straining to make my eyes see better. Did I really just see that? I cautiously started again and this time I clearly saw the bush move - and this time it grunted. I don't think I have ever screamed as loudly as it fast dawned on me that the bush was in fact a hippo and, turning smartly on my heels, I raced back to the safety of my hut, slamming the glass door shut behind me. My heart was in my mouth and pounding so hard no doubt the hippo could hear that too. Except, when I had screamed, it had scared the living daylights out of the hippo too because he had squealed like a pig at full volume and shot off in the opposite direction. Apparently, we'd caught each other out.

It soon dawned on me that a glass door wasn't going to stop an angry hippo. And so, the moment I felt I had caught my breath, I ventured back out to the veranda, sidled around the side wall to the back of my hut and, after a slow count to ten, put my head down *and ran as fast as I could to the main lodge, this time arriving without incident. I had a stiff whisky, then another; the time it took to digest just how lucky I had been.*

In Lusaka, I was told that there was bad juju in a house in which I was living and so a witch doctor was brought in to cleanse it. What I saw appear from nowhere – full on supernaturally in front of me and suspended in mid-air - was both terrifying and indescribable and the result was that my hands physically shook from the shock of it for nearly two weeks afterwards. Having spent my life always seemingly fighting something - tangible things that I could see - I was petrified to my core to now discover a whole world of intangibility that was apparently just as dangerous but which, I rationalised, I couldn't fight if I couldn't see it. For two weeks, my head was filled constantly with awful images of what might have happened and what could still happen in this new, intangible world of black magic and I couldn't stop trembling. Eventually, I had to train myself to not think about it in order to physically stop the shakes. It wasn't as easy as it may sound and took a long time and much brain-washing on my part to get the desired result. At the time, I had no idea that I was sweeping yet more mental health issues under my already jam-packed and bulging rug.

Throughout this time, no matter where I went fulfilling contracts here and there from South Africa to Kenya, I seemed to have a curious impact on the middle-aged women I met. Whether it was the woman who lived around the corner and generally looked after the house in which I stayed when in Johannesburg, or whether it was the elegant ex-Yugoslavian lady who ran a beauty salon in Nairobi, or the Finnish diplomat for whom I worked for a while on forestry and road projects in Lusaka, they all wanted to mother me. It was quite baffling really because I never asked for motherly help or advice ever. Hindsight once again tells me there must have been something in my body language, something unspoken, unwritten, and yet screaming to be heard and answered, and only the mothering sort could hear it.

While I was in Johannesburg, a white girl living opposite me was raped and killed in her own home and I shook with fear and dread as I silently waited for them to come back and finish me off too. As a foreign white girl, I had frequently been told never to go out alone because it was simply too dangerous and now this had happened to someone - just like me! - behind the fortress walls of her own barred house. As my head rationally processed the idea that home, the apparent last bastion, hadn't been safe enough to protect her, my body literally shook with fright. I couldn't sleep at night. I was haunted by imaginary fears that left me in a heightened state of paranoia. I could find no calm nor peace nor rest and so I paced endlessly around the house like the living-dead not daring to step out into the real world. The paradox was too overwhelming for me: I had cowardly opted to lock myself within the confines of a boxed home with barred windows that I knew was unable to protect me and, at the same time, I struggled to breathe, imprisoned as I was like a caged bird.

Chapter Eight: Shedding Fear

Walking without Fear or Worries

Many people are afraid to go out alone, let alone to walk. They are afraid of a variety of things: other people, animals, traffic, the rest of the world, and, more than anything else perhaps, their own thoughts. And it's not just women. A lot of people have been conditioned to fear that which is beyond our very doorstep and yet, it is my belief that walking can help us to release those fears, let them go so that we may detach ourselves from them. When we are sat in our homes, enclosed by four walls, our minds are constantly filled with thoughts and worries about past issues, present challenges or fears for the future. Indoors, we are surrounded by modern technology that feeds us bad news twenty-four hours a day and this simply fuels our fears. But when we dare to move away from the TV, the smartphones and computers, when we dare to step beyond the front door and take a walk down the road, heading off to the grey-less green of a woodland path or coastal cliff trail, we dare to open ourselves up to receiving the fresh air of the natural world, the lifeblood of the universe.

We are each different and have diverse needs and so some will want to walk further and longer in order to reach the point where we no longer have any cares or worries, fears or concerns. The more we walk, the more we shed the need to worry or fear and we no longer have time to give over to regrets. We only have the present moment to surrender to and enjoy. We don't have the time or inclination to fear anything.

In the past, when a bear or a hippo, for example, has startled me, my innate self has intuitively known that fear won't help. Rather, the question that should pose itself at times such as these is not why or how, but what do I do now? And when 'nothing' comes back as the most obvious answer, I know it is the correct answer. Fear is irrational and comes from our often morbid and yet glorious imagination. Fear is make-believe gone over the edge and so, when it comes, we must release it from our bodies and just breathe. When I screamed at the hippo in Africa, I did it with gusto and intent. There was no time to panic. Fear only attracts more fear and so, if it comes, we must dispel it instantly. When we do, we experience a feeling of unity, of oneness with all things, as though we have re-established our rightful place in the universe.

In a similar vein, one thing that keeps coming back to mind intermittently is to absolutely and consciously *not* worry about things. The more time we give to anything, the more we are likely to make it manifest. And so when we focus on something negative such as a problem or worry, we invest our energy into that problem and are more likely to make it happen than if we dismiss it outright. Nowadays, when a problem emerges, I actively choose not to think about it. I may give it the cursory, questioning: 'how do I deal with this?' And, if the solution is not immediately apparent, I put it out of my mind. I consciously choose to not dwell on it so that I am not attaching any negativity to it, trusting that the answer will come at its appropriate time, place and space, and all I have to do in between times is to remain neutral and unemotional about it.

When things seemingly go wrong, not right or, in other words, an undesired outcome has come into play in our lives, most people assume that something bad has happened or is happening and – for many – will continue to happen, a characteristic of the victim culture world in which we live. I choose to think differently these days.

The more I practise the easier I find that, when something seemingly untoward happens, I can consciously take a step back and detach myself emotionally from the so-called bad situation. If I can't make sense of it at the time, I know to be patient and accept that the sense or the reason for it will come to me eventually, as all things do. There's a reason for absolutely everything that happens in our lives and, because we may not understand the reason for it at the time, it doesn't mean that it's a bad thing. It simply means we haven't yet understood what we are meant to learn from the situation. Invariably, the answer often comes to me when I am out walking and that's why I'm happy these days not to dwell on a problem, to let things go, to know there's always good to be found in the bad, and to continue walking without worries or fears.

One day I woke up from my nightmare in Africa and I recalled confessing to myself that I was no longer living. Hiding in fear locked behind four walls, not daring to go out, not seeing anyone, was like being buried alive. So I asked myself the question, can I live like this for the rest of my life? And the answer immediately came back to me as a loud and resounding 'no'. I wanted to be free and fly like a bird. And so I decided there and then I had to be brave and to start living again. So I went and did the unthinkable. I ditched the car and I started to walk. Not just in the safe places but everywhere I'd been told not to go too. I decided to stop hiding behind the safety of the house and the car and just accept whatever life may throw at me. And you know what? I'm still alive. Nothing bad happened. Some may say I'm just lucky, others may say it's fate, but I still remember seeing the look on some people's faces as I passed them by. I saw their eyes grow wide with fright. I have absolutely no doubt that they feared me, this young white girl walking alone, because they saw in my eyes the utter absence of fear. I could hear 'wazimu' and 'mzungu' (crazy white person) whispered behind me and they would stop whatever they were doing and just stare with haunted eyes until I had passed.

I had found freedom.

So the point of all these stories? The fear and the freedom. A pattern was emerging that when I ditched the fear, I started to find my personal sense of freedom. But it doesn't just arrive and stay for good. You have to keep working at it.

In all, I spent five years in Africa before I woke up one day and knew this was not the place where I was going to spend the rest of my life. I remember sitting out by the hippo lake in a lodge in Kenya staring at Kilimanjaro in the distance. I had been sat there for some hours, thinking and contemplating my existence and my future, and wondering what I was going to do next. I sensed I was incomplete and that something had to change. I could feel the need to change drawing in as it crawled over my skin, making me itch, urging me to do something about it. I loved Africa for its rich and abundant, natural beauty but my heart knew this was not my future. Even the stand-in, would-be mothers weren't appealing enough to hold me there. I recalled sitting there, staring at the distant mountains, feeling that I had always wanted to be an explorer but that I was a hundred years too late. I sighed and got up, turned and went to pack my bag. I drove to the airport, boarded a plane and flew back to England that same night.

It was time to stop running, time to go home. Home? Funny. Maybe it was just time to go and build a home for myself. I at least recognised that my home wasn't here. I knew it was time to go back and find me.

Bears in the Woods

Recently while out walking the Sentier Cathare (a 250 kilometres hike across the south-western region of France), I was walking through a forest in the Pyrenees early one morning when a deep growl came from the dense forest undergrowth on my right-hand side, not more than five metres away from me. I stopped dead in my tracks in the instant it took for me to recognise and assimilate the sound of a bear.

For anyone who has not heard the growl of a bear before, it is a truly awe-inspiring experience. Unlike a dog which (by comparison) has a fairly shallow growl that distinctly emanates from its throat, when a bear growls, you not only hear it but you also feel it resonate deeply behind the walls of your rib cage. The growl vibrates in your heart and your chest so that the bear's implied meaning reaches your ears from within, not from without. Indeed, the bear seems to speak its language through a

different means entirely whereby you *feel* the
words and *hear* the sensations.

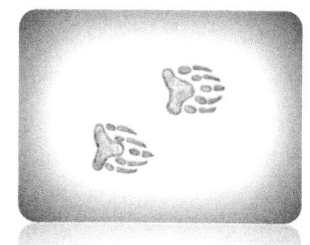

As I was admiring the beautiful feeling
of the bear's sound, I same time reached into
my pocket and pulled out a whistle which, for
some inexplicable reason, I had taken out of
my main pack and stowed in a side pocket just
the night before. Now, in the heat of the moment, I calmly and quietly
remained stationary and waited to see what would happen next. The bear
growled again a little louder but it had not shifted and so I took my cue to
move quietly onwards and away, whistle in hand, just in case. The bear
did not follow me. I had startled it and it had told me to leave in peace.

I had not panicked but my heart rate had stepped up a gear as I
had become instantly conscious and aware of the bear's presence. It was
as though my instinct was to try and tune into its frequency in order to
know what to do next. Because I was calm, it was easy to understand that
I was disturbing it and the growl was no more than my warning to move
on. I was aware that it could have attacked if it had wanted to, but part of
me intrinsically knew that it meant me no harm so long as I stayed away
from it. I had no reason to fear it. On the contrary, I think if the bear had
sensed any fear in me it could well have acted differently.

The next day, on another stage of the walk, I heard a thud and a
thump in the undergrowth and once again recognised the feel and sound
of a growling bear. I heard the lack of intention, got the message, and
carried straight on past and up the path. When I was about a hundred
metres further up, I came across a mildly, boggy part of the trail and,
clearly imprinted in the mud, were the footprints of the bear coming
down the hill in my direction. On this occasion, I knew this bear had
chosen to stay away from me.

As I continued to wend my way up the trail, my mind drifted back
to some of the near-death experiences I'd had in my life and, in that
moment, I came to the extraordinarily powerful and over-whelming

realisation that I would always be at my strongest (as Mary Shelley wrote) when I had no fear. In those situations where cool-headedness counts most, I would and could always react best if I remained fearless. This understanding was almost a feeling, a knowing, a remembering, from when I was younger that having no fear was in fact my strongest form of protection. And I really do mean having no fear, not just showing no fear; the two are very different.

When I look back on my ability to come out of dangerous experiences unscathed (shootings and car crashes, crocodiles and hippos, to name but a few), it occurs to me that what I formerly took to be naivety as having got me through a particular situation was perhaps the intrinsic knowledge of youth that simply knew that I am part of nature and, as such, have nothing to fear from it. Why should I fear what I am a part of? Besides, if it's death and dying that we're all ultimately afraid of, I'd already died once and so why on earth should I fear death in this life again? But as we get older, so our fears grow and multiply and we consequently and inevitably get hurt more and thus come to be more fearful.

But the absence of fear removes the pain.

The absence of fear is freedom.

…/…

Just as I was beginning to think the Via Aquitana would never end, a miracle happened. The road ahead suddenly dipped in front of me and, like an oasis looming on the horizon in the desert, I saw a village come shimmering into view. Church spire first and then chimneys and roofs until finally Calzadilla de la Cueza stood before me in all her glory. I licked my lips and raced on. I saw an *albergue* come into view directly in front of me and that meant a cold beer was not far behind. Walking, beer, shower, dinner, bed. My formerly complex life had been reduced to just five words.

110

Much later I came to realise that going to Africa all those years ago was the biggest run-away from myself ever. It didn't turn out to be the last either. I frequently walked off to new climes in order to escape from me. But distance not only makes the heart grow fonder, it allowed me perspective so I could see the wood for the trees. Africa was a big milestone in my life and it was precisely the right sort of medicine I needed at that point in time to help me come back to myself. Or, at least enable me to edge a little closer to reacquainting me with myself and begin to figure out just what it really was that made me tick.

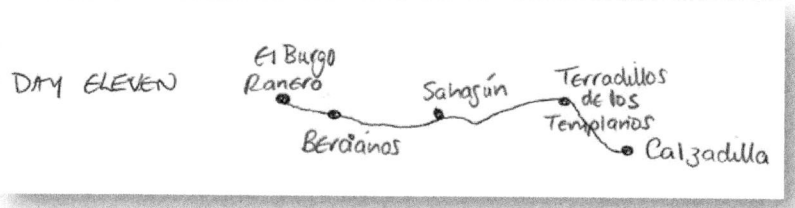

After Calzadilla, the landscape starts to change once again. I think the Via Aquitana is a rite of passage and, if you make it to Calzadilla intact, then the Camino relents thereafter and introduces a few villages intermittently along the way. It's still flat but there are generally more signs of life (passing traffic!), more villages and thus options for coffee and tortilla breaks welcomingly escalate. Nevertheless, it's boringly flat and seemingly straight and so that strange Meseta feeling of 'ever moving forward but never getting anywhere' stayed with me again throughout the day, enhanced perhaps by the fact that it also rained non-stop. Even after resting up for lunch in the busy town of Sahagún, I still couldn't shake that perturbing sentiment of forever walking on the spot and it lasted all the way to El Burgo Ranero where I finally gave in and stopped for the night.

In itself, El Burgo resembles one of those sparse and poorly populated, staging post villages that has sprouted up in the midst of a very long and empty road, spanning empty kilometres of monotonous landscape, precisely to bring relief to the poor souls who can't make it all the way to Mansilla de las Mulas or the even more ambitious destination of León. I was perhaps thinking a little unfairly when I first arrived but there didn't seem to be a whole lot of anything much going for El Burgo. Feeling sorry for myself after yet another wet and snotty-nosed, drab day, and suddenly desiring very strongly to spoil myself and have a bath rather than a shower, I decided to check into the only *hostal* I could find bearing an *abierto* sign. I opened the door and was instantly assailed by the loud buzz of a good many people excitedly laughing and chattering. So this was where all the inhabitants were hanging out!

Once up in my room, I went to run a bath only to find that the plug had been removed to deter would-be bathers. Refusing to be defeated and a little peeved at having to stuff a t-shirt into the plughole of the bath to act as a stopper, I jumped in and defiantly held it down with my heel in order to enjoy a full body soak under the comforting, warm water. I've paid for this, I thought, and so I made darn sure it worked well.

Later on that evening, I also enjoyed one of the rare evenings made marvellous when dinner turned up with green peas as a second vegetable to accompany the obligatory Camino chip. Greens on my plate! Heaven had just opened its doors once again! I thought about daring to ask for a second helping but contentedly settled for savouring every last one of the little beauties. Afterwards, as I sat in the bar sipping my wine and watching some strange Spanish game on TV that looked like handball (but I wasn't too sure how that went either), I realised that I was actually appreciating the cheerful atmosphere of that crowded place which offered a very loud and busy, but very warm and welcome, respite from the usual hush of the *albergue* after ten 'o' clock at night.

I'm sorry El Burgo Ranero for having made the rash judgement that you had nothing to offer. It turned out you gifted me one of my best feel-good Camino evenings. Had it been the ambience in the bar or the most delightful and welcome presence of the green peas?

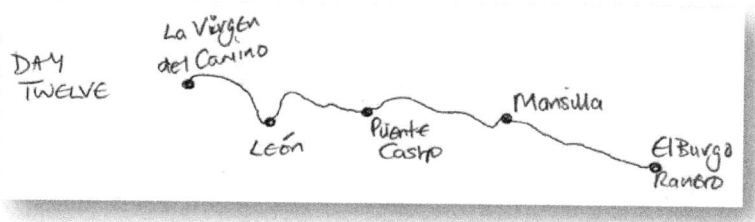

Reluctantly but dutifully I upped and offed again early the next morning, trudging out the paces, singing to myself to while away the hours, occasionally pondering the actual length of Dorothy's yellow, brick road which, I seemed to recall from the film, was not as long and straight as the Camino was proving to be on this Meseta. Having looked at the map, I knew that once I got past Mansilla de las Mulas the Camino started to climb, rising up to the Alto del Portillo, before dropping back down and into León. In my mind's eye, the sooner I got to Mansilla, the sooner the Camino would start to get interesting again.

And then a thought struck to me. I hadn't had any wow moments, pings! or startling revelations about my past for a while now. I began to speculate whether it was possible that I'd exhausted my capacity to learn anything new about myself and started to feel a little panicky and vulnerable at the thought of having possibly lost a very special and supernatural gift. I calmed myself down and rationalised that I hadn't lost anything at all. If anything, my expectations had increased to the point where I was supposing I would have a ping! moment at least once, if not more frequently, every day. But I guess life doesn't work life that. I couldn't force the revelations and I couldn't force the learning. Everything in life just happens when it's ready to happen.

This notion kept me entertained all the way up the Alto and down the other side to Puente Castro, at which point it dawned on me that I was faced with the choice of staying in León for the night or pushing onwards simply to eschew the city. Tired as I was and stubborn as always, I opted for the latter.

When I arrived at León I picked up my pace and tried to traverse the streets as quickly as I could, impatient to reach the other side where I knew the countryside would be waiting for me once more, welcoming me with a wondrous lack of deafening car horns. I stopped to take a quick photo of the cathedral – because everyone does, don't they? - and felt absolutely no desire to go in. Instead, I found a café on the outskirts of town, decided on some piquant octopus for a change to the normal tortilla, and then quickly trotted on my way out of the city via the nearest exit. I'd already decided that towns and cities were where I stopped for food and bed, but real life and all things meaningful were on the Camino, out in the countryside, away from the hustle and bustle of the mad, man-made world.

The eight and a half kilometres walk from the other side of León to La Virgen del Camino was grey and ugly. The end-of-city sprawl of identical, suburban houses, interspersed with gloomy factories, empty showrooms and sad, paint-peeled, dingy bars, was not my cup of tea. I did however love the absolute and sublime contrast of occasional grass-topped houses built into the living landscape both before and after La Virgen. Outwardly appearing to be small, one-storey caves protruding from the hillocks dotted around, they looked like they could have housed the hobbits of Hobbiton from The Lord of the Rings. I couldn't recall having ever seen them elsewhere along the Camino and so briefly pondered their significance dotted here and there in these suburbs amid such ugly, neighbouring buildings. I came up with no answers but admired the strength of character someone would have to possess to live in one.

Tired and bone-weary, I hobbled on into La Virgen where I randomly changed my routine and ate first before checking into the *albergue municipal* to shower and hopefully sleep yet another soul-filling sleep of the contented dead. While I'd stubbornly insisted on continuing to walk day after day, my cold was sapping my energy and threatening to develop into something worse again. The back of my throat still burned when I gulped and a nasty cough was desperately trying to drop into my chest. I also wondered whether a fever was trying to fight its way back into my life. When I walked into that *albergue* that night, I promised myself not to come out again until early morning the next day. And I didn't.

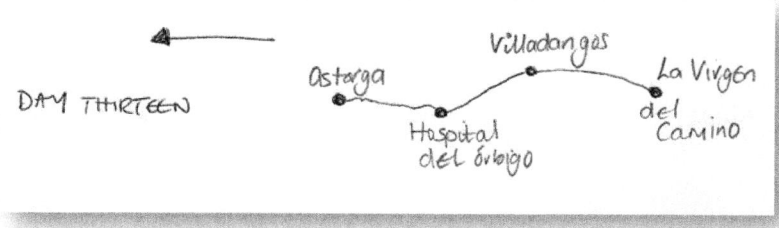

DAY THIRTEEN

The following day I arose early as usual and, always astounded at just how invigorated I could feel after only five hours of sleep, I stepped out into a surprisingly dry and thus rare and precious morning. Surreally, I walked in uneventful peace for the whole day, stopping only for a food and drink break at Hospital del Orbigo, where I lied down on a bench to bask in the sun's healing rays. The gentle heat of the sun was so medicinal that I felt fuelled by its solar energy and so, revived and raring to go, I soon pressed on, determined to reach Astorga as my next bedtime destination. But first, I had to climb the Alto de Santo Toribio which felt like a mountain after so many days spent on the flat Meseta. Once on the summit, I sat down to rest my cold-fatigued body, feet up, leaning into my backpack for cushioning against a monument bearing a black iron cross, studying Astorga in the distance. Even before I arrived at Astorga, I already felt at some level that my inner and outer landscapes would be changing once again and so resolutely decided to reach the city before nightfall. But right then, the sun was so soporific, I fell asleep for a short while and, when I was later woken by the soft cooing of pigeons, I felt somehow lighter, more peaceful and less weighed down by my cold. In fact, I didn't cough all the way into Astorga.

I absolutely loved Astorga the first time I walked through it. I don't know why because it was shut when I walked through at eight in the morning. But the second time I wandered around the place felt good too even though I couldn't pinpoint what I actually liked about it. I supposed the energies of the place must have appealed to me. All I knew was that, on both occasions, I got a real sense of wellbeing and it felt like I was about to embark on a completely different walk.

The distance from Astorga to Santiago is approximately 293 kilometres and so it's (very) roughly the last third of the Camino in terms of both time and distance. Perhaps arriving in Astorga had subconsciously felt like I was symbolically crossing a huge, mental milestone that left me feeling stronger and more at one with myself day by day. Maybe it was nothing more than the welcome relief of walking into a diverse land of green hills and snow-clad mountains after the dauntingly flat and grey Meseta days. Who knew, but I felt good there.

I stayed the night in the San Javier *albergue*, situated just around the corner from the cathedral and, as *albergues* went, it had an extravagant, almost regal, air to it. It was a beautifully maintained historic building and, not only were there only two other pilgrims staying the night (oh, yes! A possible night of snore-free sleep ahead!), but the kindly, old, care-taking volunteer in charge of that night's vigil had stoked up a storm of a fire in the huge central fireplace and sat next to it, fastidiously tending it throughout night, so that it never went out. It was Camino bliss.

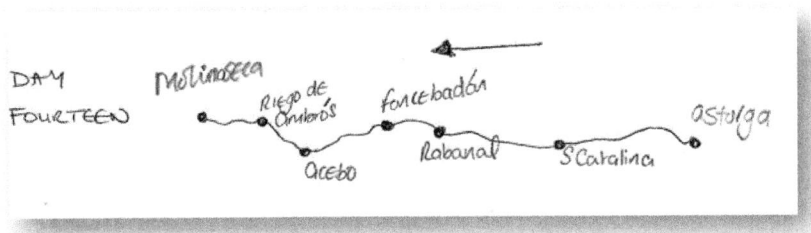

The path climbs from Astorga all the way up to Rabanal del Camino and yet the ascent felt oddly easy as though I was being gently pushed upwards and onwards all the way. The feeling, I assumed, must have been akin to experiencing one of those supposed hotspots on the planet where gravity had apparently reversed out so that it's easier to go uphill than down. In any event, ten kilometres after leaving Astorga, the beautiful village of Santa Catalina de Somoza welcomingly materialised to provide me, at the perfect time and place, with a wonderful breakfast before heading out and back up into the mountains. The open, flat lands of the Meseta and images of Dorothy and her yellow, brick road were fast becoming a distant memory.

Maybe it was because it was sunny and the air seemed to have finally warmed up a little or maybe it was because I loved the expansive views up in the mountains that I'd sorely missed during my days on the Meseta. Whatever the reason, I loved this stretch of the Camino winding up and into the quiet and attractive village of Rabanal. As usual, there was nothing open apart from one hotel offering tortilla and, taking this as a portent, I decided to stop for first lunch. In the early days soon after I left Saint-Jean-Pied-de-Port, I'd adopted the habit of resting every ten kilometres or so (or whenever I found somewhere open) to take some calories on board. At the risk of sounding like a hobbit, I actually gave each of my stops names and so, typically, the main four were: breakfast, first lunch, second lunch and dinner. I figured that walking roughly, forty kilometres a day I must be burning off around 3000 calories and, presumably needing even more energy to help my immune system stand a chance of fighting off my cold, I reckoned that I needed to refuel at every given opportunity.

As I sat there drinking my customary coffee and munching egg and potato tortilla, I mused about the upcoming village of Foncebadón made famous by legend. Every book I'd read about the Camino had spoken of and warned about the fierce dogs of Foncebadón that came out to attack and challenge any woebegone pilgrim passing through. It was a daunting prospect and I was glad that I'd brought my wooden, walking staff to Spain to keep me company along the way. I figured that even though I was probably not as spritely as the slowest of dogs, I might be able to convincingly mimic a Star Wars-type lightsaber with my staff should I have need, just to worry the pack enough to keep its distance. I stood up, shouldered my backpack and set off, scanning the trees and undergrowth lining the path, searching for wild dogs for the next five kilometres.

Vicious Animals

I love animals and I wish them no harm at all. To my mind, a life is a life and so I wish to hurt none, just as I wish none to harm me. I try to do all that I can to save the smallest as well as the largest whenever they are in need. But I guess the animal instinct in me means I will always defend myself whenever I need to. And there are certain things you can do when you encounter animals – most commonly dogs - that may be showing aggression towards you.

Depending on the nature of the animal and level of fear they possess, it will either run away or attack if you make direct eye contact with it. In Kenya, I learned not to make direct eye contact with monkeys because the group will likely attack you if it thinks you are defiantly taking it on. Conversely, if you are trying to get closer to a wild cat, a hedgehog or a bird, you should not make direct eye contact with it until you have gained its trust. Look slightly askance and approach it slowly with a soothing tone to your voice. Talk gently and calmly to it and an animal will often let you approach. Similarly, if you don't want an animal to come any closer, don't get more of its attention by eye-balling it and, most times, this will also be enough for it to move away. If you want to cross a field of cows, for example, don't walk through the middle of the herd. Calmly walk around the whole herd, making sure to give it a wide berth, and keep your eyes averted. I've stood by and watched a pack of wild boar race right past me, coming within one metre of me and, having noticed me and checked me out, not harmed me or shown any interest because I stood as still and unmoving as the trees around me.

I've often been chased by barking dogs when out running or walking past farms and it's not a nice feeling when, after you stop and turn to face them, you see them firmly planted in a hostile stance, squaring up to you, teeth bared, snarling and drooling saliva. On the plus side, you should know that if a dog is still barking at you, it is not biting you. It's either sending a warning shot that it may take a snap at you or it is still trying to suss out whether it is in fact brave enough to do so. If you bend down and pretend to pick up a stone, it's often enough to make a wary dog retreat out of fear. If the dog continues to come at you, hesitantly and yet still barking, it is apprehensive and may try nip at your heels if you turn and leave. So stand tall and shout at it aggressively calling its bluff. Point at it, look it straight in the eye and tell it to sod off. You can even stamp your foot which usually has the effect of making it retreat a step or two. When you see it step back, you know you have it licked and so continue until it has lost its nerve completely and turns to go away. Shouting loudly also has the bonus effect of bringing attention to the owner of the dog if he or she happens to be around and, when they are, they invariably do come to bring the dog to heel.

If, however, the dog falls quiet with its teeth clearly bared and no owner has arrived, it has become quite serious about having a bite. The alternative then – or perhaps the last resort even - is to rise up, making yourself as big and daunting as you possibly can, roar as loudly as you can at it waving your arms and making such a racket that the dog (which didn't see this counter attack coming) is now afraid of you. Now you have to look it in the eye and show it no fear. You have to mean it, shout at it and believe it to make the dog back down. The absolutely last thing you should do in this situation is turn and run. It will come for you. Instead, you would do well to smartly find a big stick or stones with which to defend yourself.

In doing all of the above at one time or another, I have never experienced a vicious dog stay and persist in attacking. Most wild animals only attack if they are hungry or feel threatened. Most other animals attack only when they are utterly desperate or feel confident they have the upper hand. If an aggressive animal cannot sense fear in you, this in itself will make it wary of you. The key then is to have no fear. Having no fear will make an aggressive animal fearful of you and a passive animal will remain thoroughly indifferent.

Foncebadón – So where were the vicious dogs? As I trudged through the one and only street in the hamlet (made haunting and eerie only by the absence of any form of life whatsoever), I was instantly aware that there really was nothing out of the ordinary here. It was quiet but there were a couple of *albergues* and a few shops open which was already a whole lot more than some of the other villages that I'd passed through along the way. As I was climbing up the winding path out of the village heading towards La Cruz de Ferro, I became conscious that something was gnawing at me, making me itch under my skin, and the peculiar notion came to me that I'd been cheated. Strange. Why cheated? Instead of looking at the hill ahead of me, I turned my eyes downwards to gaze at the snow on the path and listen to the rhythmic crunching made by each slow and steady, trudging footfall of my boots. Stomp, stomp, cheated, cheated. Why cheated? Something was tapping at my brain and I couldn't quite place it. I reached the summit and before I disappeared over the brow into the woods ahead, I paused and turned, relishing the opportunity for a moment's respite in which to catch my breath and admire the vast lands of the province of León disappearing far below and behind me. I was so high up now that I towered over the hills and valleys that had already appeared to me as mere specks in the distance when I'd set off earlier that morning. I huffed and I puffed, my lungs desperately sucking in the oxygen from the thin mountain air, and I waited for my heartbeat to slow back down to its normal rate. It was then that I had my ping! moment.

.../...

Chapter Nine: Waking Up

Back in England, I married a guy. Eighteen months later, I divorced another.

While I was out in Africa I had sold my flat in London and so coming back to England with my suitcase meant I had to start life from scratch. Initially, I went to stay at my parents' small hotel in Cornwall while I looked for a job. This didn't last long. I had learned how to find some inner peace while living and walking alone in Africa but, back sharing a house with my parents again, the old tensions started to re-emerge and so I settled for the first job I could find which offered me back my all-important space. It was a mistake. I held that job in Bristol for five years but it damn near drove me insane. It was a marketing role in a business-to-business computer company that was so unsuitable for me I hated every minute of it. And, because I was unhappy in the role, it brought out that old defensive protection mechanism within me - my faux friend anger - which had me snapping at people when I should have been patient, and which was, in reality (I see now), nothing other than a mirror image of me snapping at myself for persisting in a job that I hated. But, my primary job search criterion at that time was money and, since I couldn't find another job that paid as well, I did as I used to do in those years, I stuck it out and it tore my soul apart.

But, in between times, I haven't mentioned that I'd met someone while I was out in Africa and, after I came back to the UK, being of a certain age and closer to family influences once again, there was a certain amount of pressure on me to not become an old maid, do the decent thing, get married, settle down and start my own home. So I ended up doing just that. Or at least I tried. Despite my soul screaming at me that it was the wrong thing to do (and I remember quite vividly hearing my heart scream nooooo! so loudly it reverberated throughout my entire body), I married the guy I had met in Africa. Initially we bought a house in the suburbs of Bristol thinking this would be ideal for both of us from a work point of view. What I soon came to discover however was that, whereas I liked the house, I could no longer tolerate living in the city. Leaving London to go and live in Africa had been a relatively easy transition for me and I'd not given it much thought. Coming back and trying to settle into a city environment again was a living hell. I couldn't sleep at night for the noise. Not noise for noise's sake because there's no such thing as silence in my view. What troubled me were the harsh sounds of people screaming and crying, traffic tearing past the house in the middle of the night, horns honking in the distance. I'd become a different person while living in Africa and I couldn't bear living in such a noisy and built-up environment anymore.

Perhaps this is one of the reasons why our marriage only lasted eighteen months. I couldn't stand the city and so we moved to a small, remote village in the Forest of Dean. It suited me perfectly. Finally, here was a house where the energies felt so right that I believed I could come to call this one a home. Whether it suited my husband or not, I don't know, because we never talked. Or should I say he never talked. He presumably thought I spoke too much but I could never get him to speak his mind or engage him in conversation that didn't revolve around the banal. I got tired of not being able to share anything, I felt cut off and cut out and this, coupled with the drain of a job I didn't like, took me slumping over yet another edge. Our marriage wasn't working. It was a disaster.

The guy who I had first met loved the outdoors, fitness and walking. He was happy and fun, always telling jokes and loved being in the company of others. The guy I was now married to now was an inert blob, stuck to his computer at every given minute of the day and no longer interested in anyone or anything else, including me. It tore me apart. I was confused as to how and why the person I married could transform into the complete opposite of what I had believed him to be. It was as though signing the marriage certificate, a mere piece of paper, had compelled him to undergo a complete personality change.

I believe there are two sides to every coin and so I don't want to whinge about my ex-husband or blame him for our failed marriage. Just as it transpired he wasn't right for me, I'm sure as hell if he was honest and would have talked about it he would have realised that I wasn't right for him. There were no doubts that I had changed too. Certainly in Africa he wouldn't have seen the latent anger in me waiting to ignite when someone lit my short fuse. But if he had issues with me, he never said. He never told me what he thought and so I was always left to brew my own paranoid thoughts. We no longer had common interests and never saw each other. In fact, it was like sharing a house with a roommate that you never saw because he never came out of his room. It was eerie to say the least. I felt single again because I was always left doing things - like living life! - alone. I felt betrayed and cheated – Cheated! That was it! There was the missing link!- as though I had been conned into marrying one person and now had to live with another by trickery or deceit like in some bad fairy tale. It was beyond dreadful; it was intolerable. Eventually, I remember waking up in bed one morning and asking myself the questions: Can I do this for the next forty years? More to the point, do I want to do this for the next forty years?

No!!!! was the resounding silent scream in my head.

So when he came home from work one day I caught him before he made it up to the computer room. I told him that after eighteen months of being married to this strange new fella I would not spend the rest of my life married to him. And so I ended it. And the relief I felt flooding through my body, the release of so much pent-up tension, was instant and long overdue. It was as though I'd been holding my breath for... eighteen months?

My husband moved out the same night and splitting up and settling our differences was all very straight forward because we hadn't

been together for that long. He didn't ask for anything nor did he contest
anything and so we simply halved everything.

In hindsight, it's easy to say that if it's not right or forced, it won't
work. But, at the time, those too-easy-to-conjure-up self-deprecating
doubts crept back and I blamed myself for having screwed up yet again. I'd
gone and ruined everything and here was yet another happy ever-after
potential gone to waste. Back came those old paranoias: lack of self-
esteem and self-worth. I embarked on a series of casual and careless
relationships that, at the time, I would have said were meaningless.
Reflection tells me they were careless at a superficial level but,
subconsciously, I'd only ever been looking for love. And yet, every time
someone tried to do just that, just love me, each time a relationship was
starting to show signs of looking good, I ended up pushing my partner
away and closing things down. Unconsciously I pushed them away,
sometimes I even consciously pushed them away, but always it was
because I was afraid. My mind teemed with those childhood experiences,
emotions, memories, and conclusions about being unworthy of being
loved, and so I pushed away love before it stood a chance of hurting me
deeply. In truth, my mind-frame was that love hurt too much and I didn't
want to be hurt any more. Hence the series of relationships became
meaningless. I was meeting people and pushing them away. My own
vicious circle was fuelled by wanting love, fearing love, wanting love,
fearing love, and so it went on.

My life was going nowhere and my depression was deepening
fast. The black hole of my childhood fears had somehow made it back into
my life and I was tumbling down it, wheeling blindly and headfirst, utterly
unaware and out of control.

.../...

I smiled to myself and turned my attention back to the path and
the thought of La Cruz de Ferro that I knew lay ahead at an altitude of
1,505 metres. Despite my vertigo, I loved climbing mountain paths and so
this was hugely enjoyable for me. Steep up-hills make the breath harder

to find which forced me to dig harder. As my breathing became deeper and my climbing pace more regular, I recognised that familiar sensation of pure joy infiltrate my every body cell. Climbing up beautiful mountain paths, breathing in the crisp, dry air and feeling the ice-cold tingle on my cheeks, seeing myself surrounded by beauty with every step, I knew that life couldn't get more honest than that. It was pure and simple. Walking in nature and just being here right now was all so simple, so honest. Nothing hurt and no-one was trying to hurt anyone. I felt good, I felt fresh, lighter and cleansed, and such an over-whelming sense of happiness surged in my chest that it brought tears to my eyes. I wasn't being cheated. Not now, not then, not ever. Life had only ever played out what it had to in order to get me moving on again and become more aware of the need to change. For a while, I had being doing all the wrong things, trying to live a life that just wasn't meant to be and, as such, it had to end. I had to move on to the next stage.

I grinned and picked up my pace looking forward to the vista that was waiting for me at La Cruz de Ferro. I glanced skyward and saw that I'd have to hurry my step a little because it looked like more snow was on its way.

As it turned out, after reaching the summit and coming down the other side of the Alto Altar, it was as though the snow clouds had been held back on the other side because, on this side, the sun was out, beaming brightly and looking as though it had been patiently waiting for me to show up. It was sunny and warmer than I had so far felt on this cold and wintry Camino. In fact, it was so unseasonably warm that, I realised too late, the tip of my left ear that was always sun-facing as I continued my westward walk to Santiago had now burnt. I wrapped a scarf around my head, turban-style, to protect my ear from further damage as the sun continued to bear down relentlessly and the irony didn't fail to hit me. A rare period of warmth on this Camino journey and I was forced to wear a scarf around my head which had me sweating profusely. Stop grumbling, I told myself. The sun and the sweating would be good to cure my cold, I reasoned. As it turned out and much to my chagrin, I had to wear that scarf for several days more. I'd never been a dapper dresser but the Camino frequently had me dressed in such a ridiculous state as I attempted to protect myself against the extremes of the varied weather conditions with such a limited wardrobe to hand.

The huge downhill descent from the Alto made it all the more easy to glide down into Molinaseca under the weight of my backpack. It wasn't that the terrain wasn't challenging, it mostly certainly was. I needed to keep my wits about me to avoid slipping over for the scree was heavily coated in a thick layer of crystal, white snow and it proved to be a seriously steep slide all the way down to Acebo. Thank goodness I had my wooden staff to keep me upright on no end of precarious skids and slides. But, I wasn't exerting any effort in climbing and so the afternoon's downhill meant a different muscle group in my legs was being employed. The effect was like gifting a period of rest and recuperation to my sore calves and thighs.

Darkness was creeping in by the time I arrived in Molinaseca and so I headed for the first open *albergue* I could find. After yet another colossal day's walk, I was ready for food and bed at the earliest opportunity. My mind briefly flitted back to my earlier thoughts about my broken-down marriage and the drawn-out period of depression that ensued. Funny, I thought, how radically different my life was now, being both stress-less and care-free, to how it used to be way back then. How did I ever let myself become so depressed?

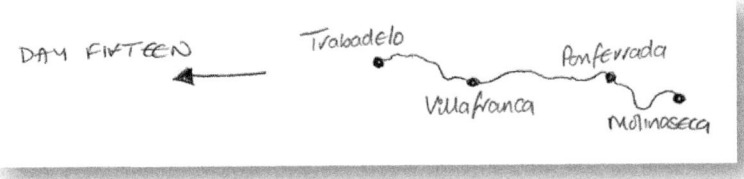

The downhill continued the next morning as I left Molinaseca at dawn with my tender ear wrapped up in a scarf once more. From up the hill, the sight of the sprawling city mass that was Ponferrada, with all its industrial chimneys belching out sickly, yellow smoke into the clear mountain air had not been pleasant. So I hunkered down and picked up my stride, determined to clear the city as fast as possible.

And so I breezed down and into Ponferrada and was sitting down for breakfast tortilla and coffee before the heat of the sun had truly kicked in. It's true that Ponferrada was yet another big town but actually, once I was in it, I thought it was quite pretty with its gardens and parks, monuments and historic cobbled walkways. There were a few occasions when I had to resist the urge to panic because I'd temporarily lost sight of the Camino arrows while trying to exit the place. But that had happened in every city and so I knew now to stay calm in the full and certain knowledge that the countryside was waiting for me just beyond the city limits. And so it was and so it remained, as I spent the next few hours passing through small (closed) villages, up quiet streets and alongside open fields, all the uneventful way onwards and up into Villafranca del Bierzo.

I think it must have been a religious holiday the day I arrived in Villafranca because the locals were out in force celebrating in the streets. The bars and restaurants were packed and I'm pretty sure it wasn't to celebrate the return of the sun. I sat down at a table in a sunny spot in the main square and waited for the waitress to come and take my staple order for coffee and potato tortilla. To hell with that, I thought, it's sunny. I'll have a cold beer instead. And I sat and watched the world go by as I enjoyed the brief moment of re-contact with society and watching the busy-ness of happy people.

Before too long, I heard a voice close by and pulled myself back from my reverie. "Excuse me?" I said. A fellow pilgrim wanted to share the table and I welcomed him to sit. And the inevitable questions followed: How far had I walked that day? Wasn't the weather amazing? Hadn't it been dreadful so far? When did I start the Camino? Where from? How had I found the *albergues* in Astorga? Wasn't the cathedral fantastic? Wasn't the cathedral at Burgos lovely?

127

It was when the conversation started to take on a religious tone that I decided to step up and be heard. I confessed that I hadn't been into any church or cathedral on the Camino so far. Back came the quasi-expected retort, "But you must have! Otherwise what was the point of doing the Camino de Santiago at all?" I decided not to respond and turned back to concentrate on my cold beer instead. So the barrage of questions continued: Did I walk alone? What? Always? Wasn't the point of the Camino to be sociable and meet new people? What time did I set off on a morning? Where was I aiming for that night? Obviously a lonely walker who doesn't like being by himself, I thought.

I decided to have another go and told him I was headed for Trabadelo. "No way," came the reply. "If you stopped at Molinaseca last night that means it'll be almost forty kilometres. You can't do that. No one does that." To which I told him that I'd been averaging thirty-five to forty kilometres every day from the start. "No way," he repeated. "You can't." I stared him coolly in the eye. There wasn't any point in saying anything. Since I'd first taken the bus from Bayonne to get to Saint-Jean-Pied-de-Port, everyone I met who asked the question about daily distances told me that forty a day was impossible and, more to the point, that I couldn't do it. And every time I heard it, it rankled me. Why? Because not one of these people knew me. They knew absolutely nothing about me, about who I was and what I did for a living, and here they all were telling me what I could and couldn't do and indirectly accusing me of being a liar.

My fellow pilgrim must have felt uncomfortable with my silence or my stare or both and so he soon bade me a *Buen Camino*, upped his pack and went on his way. Presumably further down the village where he could find a more sociable pilgrim to chat with. I turned back to the sun, shut my eyes, and breathed deeply and slowly into my stomach. I felt myself ping! back to another time and event.

Chapter Ten: The Next Ordeal

When I met the next man of my dreams I was so buoyant, so upbeat, I felt I had a new reason to enjoy living again. The mistake almost killed me.

The culminating point in my seemingly on-hold-going-nowhere life was an extremely destructive relationship with someone who I had been working with at that miserable, computer workplace in Bristol. We both ended up leaving the place for better jobs and, agreeing we were in a partnership now, he moved into my house. Things seemed to be going well for, oh, a couple of weeks, before questions about where I was going or what I was doing, and with whom, suddenly started to arise.

I had always thought that I was pretty strong-minded, that I made my own decisions and was very hard to be deceived but, actually, reflection says that, even in my childhood, my teachers would say that I was easily led astray. If someone said black I might say white just because I could. But if someone said try this or why not do that, nine times out of ten I would, just for the experience. I had always been very open-minded. Or was it gullible? Or both?

But the story went something like this.

This man was always right. I was always wrong. Whatever I was doing soon enough and sure enough would be wrong. He would not be happy. I would have caused that unhappiness. More than that, I would have intentionally made him unhappy. I would try to make amends to bring happiness back into the relationship. This would make things worse. I would be purposefully making things worse. He would walk out. I would be left wondering if he'd ever come back and what I could do to bring him back. And so on.

Our relationship was full of anger and destruction, the constant coming together and falling apart, explosive arguments and accusations, both of us so full of paranoia, anger and mistrust. It served to fuel my anger button... a lot. After too much prodding and poking, I would go wild, shaking and seething with anger as I screamed my innocence. He would explain how I was always the problem because of my anger. I would then feel guilty, caught red-handed being angry, all the while ashamed knowing that anger wasn't the way to resolve this anyway. I was so frustrated that he couldn't hear me, wouldn't listen to me or believe me when I protested my good intentions. He wouldn't accept it. He was always right. I was always wrong. He was not happy. This was my fault. And so the cycle continued.

Whereas I accept that there are always two sides to a coin, I am happy to summarise the man as a complete control freak. Many would say that it takes one to know one and I agree. But I have always had the belief and the awareness to refrain from telling other people what to do because I don't like it when people tell me what to do. In this particular scenario, what my partner had actually been doing to me was removing the remnants of any self-belief that I still had about myself, any last fragments of self-worth. He just took it all away with his clever words and turn of phrase, leaving me to believe that I was an evil, worthless person. It was done so slowly, on the drip, I didn't see it coming. How could I possibly not have recognised there was even a problem? Not realised the damage he was doing to me or, more correctly, I was letting him do to me? I guess I spent so much time trying to make things right, trying to make things better, that I was changing myself constantly without ever really being aware, always trying so hard to placate him and make him see me in a different light. I felt so ashamed that I was apparently ruining this relationship too that I saw less and less of my friends and made excuses as often as I could. I was too embarrassed and too afraid to admit that, after having screwed up my marriage, this relationship was now also very rocky Yet again, it was all my fault. And so I started to hide from them, my friends and my family, and the world, fearing them all and their inevitable condemnation and judgement to follow.

I eventually lost my job because I simply couldn't function properly in the role anymore. I obviously wasn't seeing what was (and later became) apparent to everyone else. For anyone out there, male or female, who has ever had this experience, you'll understand me when I say that it feels as though your have been brutally torn open head to toe and left sorely raw and exposed, every remaining ounce of self-belief ripped out of you to be replaced with feelings of absolute meaninglessness, self-hate, worthlessness, confusion, internal conflict, self-disgust, guilt, shame... And the condemning list goes on.

One day, it got to the point where I physically couldn't go through with the usual scenario of events yet again. One more argument, one more torment, and I was vomiting. It made me physically sick to go through this, day after day, time and time again, and my head ached so badly, crammed as it was with such destructive emotions. I asked him to leave, this time for good. I didn't have the mental or physical strength to cope with him anymore. Up until this point there had only been one occasion in which he had physically hurt me, bruising my wrists with the force of his grip while trying to prevent me from leaving the house. In this instance, giving him the ultimate goodbye, he must have known I meant it because he became so enraged that he held me up by my throat against a wall, hanging me, dangling me, choking me, while he ranted and raged about how I was the nastiest piece of work he had ever met. He eventually ran out of steam and left me there, fragile and broken on the floor. My throat was tender and bruised for days but, despite the fear, it had given me the strength to me make my decision final.

I eventually got him evicted from my house but, even after seeking legal intervention that led to a restraining order being put in place, he would still come back to torment me and flaunt the legal order. I had had enough. Even with him physically removed, he was constantly taunting me: sitting in his car outside my friends' houses while I visited them; following me on the motorway; re-arranging or breaking the garden furniture while I was out; sending condemning letters via his solicitor threatening to take my house away. Wherever I went, he was lurking somewhere. I became sick with paranoia and unable to sleep or eat. I lived in constant fear that he was going to pop up somewhere, at some time when I was alone and vulnerable, but this time I imagined the situation would be much worse as he would finally have the chance to vent all his built-up anger out on me.

But that moment didn't arrive. Instead, there came an awakening, or rather a moment, when I realised that I had lost myself and I couldn't see the point in living anymore. I had become nothing more than a scared empty shell, a brainless husk, and I had nothing left to give, not even to myself. I got to that point where, emotionally, I was so spent there was nothing left to feel for myself, let alone anyone else. I had become numb in both body and brain. I was so void of feeling it made me physically weary and I lacked the energy to do anything at all.

And, just when I thought it couldn't evolve further, it did. I became sick to death, not just of him, but of all people, of love and of life not working out. I felt so sick and yet so empty to the extent that I didn't want to continue living anymore. I remember thinking that, all my life, I had been as solid as a rock, holding it together for all those years, trying to exist peacefully, all the while looking for that elusive friend called Happiness. And now I was reduced to this husk that couldn't eat anymore, couldn't walk, couldn't think, couldn't talk. I couldn't even be angry and I couldn't feel fear. There was nothing left in me.

Then one morning, after yet another soul-wrenching, sleepless night, I knew that I didn't want to live like this anymore. I duly went out and climbed up the bank into the woods that backed on to my garden with the intention of not coming back. I found and sat down on a big rock and, in the height of my numbness, started shutting down like an animal. I knew no-one would interrupt me because people didn't go there. Only the badgers and foxes and they wouldn't bother me.

But I'd had enough of life and I was sure I knew just how to die.

For anyone who has ever shared a similar experience (and I'm sure there any many), you know what it's like. For those who have not, please forgive me, it's hard to put into words. The absolute emptiness, the sheer hopelessness that brings on a numb detachment where you cannot see how you can do any more, you are no longer interested in life or living or breathing. Nothing touches you because you have become so cold, so numb, so removed from everything living and vital. This is the point I had reached when I went out and sat on the rock to die. I couldn't care less about anything or anyone else because I couldn't even care about me.

.../...

I smiled a little wryly to myself as I stood, donned my backpack, and began the long and winding climb up to Trabadelo. If I was lucky enough the sun would be still out when I arrived so I could eat out later on. As I walked, I mused about how I was much more careful these days about believing what people said about me, especially when they didn't know me. I'd even learned to evaluate better what family and friends said about me so that I wouldn't fall into the same traps of damaging mind-games. Some people aren't aware of what they say and do, but others are, and it's this latter lot who are the dangerous ones. But, more importantly, what I came to learn for myself is that it is absolutely no-one else's fault what happens to you in life. You cannot blame someone else for the way you feel or what you do. You bring it on yourself. If you let it happen. Awareness versus unawareness is a choice that many people are still unaware of in this victim-conscious world.

I'd chosen to stop at Trabadelo on purpose because it was not far from the foot of the big monster of a mountain, O'Cebreiro. Today I would walk up the giant 1,310 metres high mountain and down the other side, out of Castilla y Léon into Galicia and onwards to Triacastela. This was the second time I would be tackling this mountain and so I knew the last eight kilometres up to the summit and village of O'Cebreiro were steep and tough. It was going to be a very arduous and sweaty morning's climb.

In the early hours of the morning, the steady hike up to Herrerías (the real foot of the mountain) was cool and enjoyable. The clear blue skies told me it was going to be a hot and sunny ascent up to O'Cebreiro and so I stopped for a coffee to gee myself up for the big one. And O'Cebreiro was big. With the building heat of the day, coupled with the already apparent stillness of the breeze, the atmosphere was stifling. As I huffed and puffed my onward and upward way to the summit, mostly looking down at my feet in case I psyched myself out, I plodded like a pack mule, step after slow step, fortunately in the shade of the wooded trail, listening to my breath, focusing on its regularity, stopping only when I needed to pause for more oxygen and to wipe the sweat from my eyes.

It was a beautiful part of the Camino, there were no doubts about that. It was physically tough and demanding even of the fittest, but it gave truly inspiring, intermittent views out over the disappearing valleys of Castilla y Léon already trodden and left behind and I relished every minute of my tranquil interaction with nature in those parts. The trees in the bordering woods were so evidently ancient and so tangibly alive. Even the fields reserved for livestock oozed a primordial vitality out of the land and into the air. I loved Galicia. There must have been an energetic pull that resonated deeply within me because I sensed something enormously vibrant in the mountains of Galicia that had me feeling buoyant and energised wherever I walked. It was as though the living landscape itself was speaking to me, calling me, wanting to tell me its secrets, and I couldn't get enough of it. It was magical.

The Centaur

When I first moved to France it occurred to me that, throughout my entire life, I had always gone off exploring other parts of the country (and other countries) but I had never taken the time to explore the lands on my very doorstep. Odd perhaps, I don't know. But I vowed to start spending a lot more of my time discovering the area I had just moved into: the Razès. Characterised by beautiful rolling hills and valleys swathed in sunflowers in summer and wavering wheat in winter, the Razès offers panoramic views of the mysterious Montagne Noire to the north, the Malepère Massif to the east, the impressive Pyrenees to the south and the arable farming lands of the Ariège to the west. I fell in love with the Razès for its wide-ranging diversity of flora and fauna, vineyards and scrubland, forests and farms, birds of prey and orchids.

And just two kilometres away down a country path is the Bois d'en Bas: a fairly dense woodland perhaps eight kilometres square. I'd been living in the Razès for several years before I eventually summoned the wherewithal to sate my curiosity and enter the woods. Initially, I created a looping circuit of one kilometre, then two, then three, gradually expanding my loop over time in order to explore more of the unmapped woods without getting lost.

One day, I chose to follow a track that was new to me and barely discernable due to the encroaching dense undergrowth. I was alone as usual (I never met anyone in the woods) when suddenly I sensed an enormous, almost majestic, presence materialise right beside me. This new energy force standing on my left side was huge and I felt part of it flowing into and through me. I cannot explain it better other than to say that my immediate sensation was that something or someone had just appeared from nowhere and was now standing right next to me, invisible to my sight, but otherwise very, very tangible. People say the woods have eyes and everywhere you go there are undoubtedly birds and animals surveying your every move. But it was the wrong time of year for the mating deer or wild boar to be close by, and they would have anyhow made themselves visible.

I fail to express adequately in words how palpable the energy emanating from this presence felt as it permeated my own body and aura, moving through me in waves that seemed to ebb and flow. As the energy pulsated, I had a sudden appreciation of the nature of the presence stood next to me and the word that trickled from my lips was 'centaur'.

Within a flash, I knew with the utmost certainty that a centaur had joined me and he was there to protect me with the cloak of his own life-force as I walked through this particular part of the woods. In the twinkling of an instant, I had no doubts at all about how he looked, what his purpose was, and how honoured I was to be in the presence of such a magnificent being. We continued to advance down the track walking side by side until, where the path began to broaden out and merge with a wider trail that I recognised, the centaur and his energies disappeared as swiftly as they'd arrived.

Needless to say, I kept going back to that very spot because I always wondered if he was still around; but I've not seen or felt him since that incident. And the more I read and understand about nature spirits, it would appear that you can't just call on them to manifest since they are not at our beck and call. I surmised from the experience that the centaur came and offered me his protection for a particular moment and purpose in time – I don't know why - but he wasn't going to come and show himself again just because I wanted him to. To this day, I still send thanks to him every time I think of the instance, just as I give thanks to all the nature spirits and guides who look after me wherever I go.

When I summited O'Cebreiro the first time I walked the Camino, I was a little shocked, if not mildly disappointed. After having spent some hours walking through some of the most serene and stunningly, beautiful countryside on the Camino so far, I emerged into a small but extremely noisy village, bustling with coachloads of tourists. There were bars and restaurants, a couple of *albergues* and some tacky memento shops that I'd not experienced before on the Camino, presumably with it being winter. I really felt quite disoriented, a little confused and out of place. I bought a cold beer, an excuse to sit for a short while as I quenched my thirst, and sat in anonymity on a picnic bench where I had the best vantage to study the mad throng of happy day-trippers from a distance.

I can't have spent more than fifteen minutes idling there before I impulsively grabbed my backpack and headed out of the village, back into the calming coolness of the woodlands, to escape the thronging mass of noisy people. I was heading for Triacastela and, while it meant another four hours of walking ahead, I was happy to keep going and put some distance between me and the tourism frenzy.

A little more than four kilometres outside of O'Cebreiro I reached the Alto do San Roque and the huge Monumento do Peregrino, the pilgrim monument, perched high on a rock overlooking the verdant valleys of Galicia below stretching out into the distance as far as the eye could see. Perfect! The sun was out, it was warm and windless: the perfect spot for a short and peaceful rest. I nestled into the sandaled feet of the giant pilgrim statue as he timelessly strode forever westwards to Santiago. And, mimicking my stone friend, I also raised my hand to shield my eyes, straining to see as far as I could into that far and distant future that was just waiting ahead of me. Ping!

Chapter Eleven: Rebirth

I died and was born again.

I sat down to die. To shut my body down, bit by gradual bit, until the remnants of any breath were simply squeezed out of my empty body. I think I might have spent about four or five hours sat on that rock; it could have been longer. I don't really know because I had no concept of time, either before or after. I was just there, not thinking, doing nothing other than willing my body to shut down. Stop living. Stop breathing. Stop being. My only intention in going there had been not to come back. And I died.

But I'm recalling this to you now and so I obviously did come back. But the come-back was truly one of the strangest experiences I have ever had in my life. I was dead... until... through my numb oblivion, an electric force of a cosmic punch surged through my body and smacked me hard in the solar plexus. I heard the words as my body felt the message and it still rings out through me today:

"Get up, you are a survivor, you will go on."

In hindsight, I can only surmise that I must have been so utterly emptied of everything that my guardian angel, God, or some other universal being, decided to step in and save me. I recall this incredible sensation, a punch to the stomach from the inside out, and there were the words. Actually, I didn't hear the words, I felt the words:

"Get up, you are a survivor, you will go on."

I was stunned. So utterly and absolutely astonished. And alive. I had been so empty, so nothing, for so long and now suddenly there was this vibrant feeling of life magically coursing through my body once again. A sensation so overwhelmingly powerful that it had penetrated through the numbness that nothing else could. There was no-one else around. No-one, nothing, apart from the forest, the rock and me. But I had heard it so loud and so clearly. It was oh, so tangible, oh, so physical. But how could it be? It had come from deep within me and woken up some part of my dying awareness. It had been mighty enough to breach the black hole of my weary mind that had been free-falling in fatal oblivion and it was now shining forth the brightest beacon of light and hope. The words vibrated throughout my body with such utter clarity and they kept resonating for some time more, filling me with a renewed sense of life and energy.

"Get up, you are a survivor, you will go on."

The message was simple and commanding. There were no questions and I had no doubts and so I responded. I got up. I stood up and I felt better. I was somehow lighter, instantly and very noticeably absent of worries, cares and concerns, not in a dangerous 'I don't care anymore' way, but in a 'there is nothing to worry about' sort of way.

I floated back down through the forest to my house and the place suddenly took on a very different feel. I felt as though I had just been cocooned, protected by some sort of invisible cloak of strength, because suddenly nothing around me about the house, my failed relationships, people I did or didn't know, my entire life, nothing touched me. Nothing hurt and yet I knew I was no longer numb. There was no pain, no anger, no negative feelings, only a strange, calming sense of peace and an inner happiness that I'd never experienced before. I was tranquil and serene and I liked this feeling a lot.

Whatever had filled me with a renewed sense of life had me walking as though I was on cloud nine for all of the next year. I smiled serenely, I felt calm and peaceful, I could laugh again and I found joy in everyone and everything. No issue was an issue any more; nothing was a problem. I drifted easily through life, as I now reflect, living in the present moment where nothing from the past hurt me and nothing about the future worried me. I genuinely felt born again. Not really as a new me but *as the me that should have or could have been all along. It was the only way I could sum up the experience: reborn. How odd?*

Never having been a religious person and not believing in the church, it was distinctly odd but the phrase that kept coming back to me was that I had been born again. It was as if I had been emptied of all my past and the future and had been stood back on the planet – this time upright and a bit more together - to learn from this experience and to give life another go.

But this time, I was to have a stab at living life properly, the way it was meant to be lived. Some part of me intrinsically knew that when I went out to die on that rock, it was a cry from my soul to give up the miserable life I had been suffering, the life I didn't want. Coming back to life was all about finding the happy and love-filled life that I did want. I knew that it was time for me to stop running for there really was nowhere to hide. It was time for me to be honest and start taking a good and close look at myself. I knew it would take a lot of strength and determination but, if I truly wanted to be happy, I would have to work hard at it and so I needed to know more about being sad. More specifically, I needed to research the whole field of mental illness.

I started to read about anxiety and depression – and was taken aback to be able to identify with many of the signs and symptoms - and naturally came to hear about depersonalisation disorder. The continuous experience of feeling detached and emotionless as though I was living in an unreal, vacuous world – it sounded precisely like where I had been. How did that happen, by the way? One day I was okay and the next I wasn't. It had silently crept up on me, slowly seeping into my skin, my every muscle and sinew, until one day it had taken over and I was no longer me. I was it. Depersonalisation disorder. In truthful retrospect, I think – no, I know – that I'd turned a blind eye and looked the other way when I saw the ominous and very real signs of a break-down coming. My mind's self-defence mechanism had, for a long time, kept me in denial. If I was ever going to recover from this and lead a truly, happy life, I knew I would have to stop denying the past and look for a different solution to life and living in the future.

And so my neglected walking life was born again. Well, after a short while. After coming back from Africa, I had thrown myself into work and, feeling I was too busy and didn't have the time, I had stopped walking as a result. Now, after the rock experience, in the initial months, I ran and ran and ran because it served a multitude of purposes: it gave me the time to reflect and come back to myself at a time when I was busy with work; it burnt off my excess energy so that I always felt calmer; it completely dissipated my anger; it made me open my eyes to the outer world so I did not morbidly focus on my inner world. Three or four times a week, I would go out running in the woods behind my house and enjoy the sights, the smell and the feel of the forest as though it was the first time, every time I went out. I used to run until I was spent, taking comfort in the sound of my huffing and puffing because then I knew I was alive and kicking. I wasn't afraid to push myself hard because, having died and been reborn, I was now thirsty for life.

But I ran too hard one day and ripped a hamstring so badly that I couldn't walk for several days. It took some months to eventually get out running again, but my body started to suffer in other ways and other places because I focused on nothing else but the running. A physio told me I needed to 'balance myself' and so I broadened my range and took up swimming and cycling which helped. But, whatever I did, I always preferred to do it alone because I loved the time, the space and the breath it gave me to be able to discover more about me. In isolation, I found that I could reflect openly and honestly on aspects of myself and my experiences, learn from them, repair and move forward as a more composed and cohesive person. It was at this point that I started to walk again, proper walking, through the woods away from the village and people so that I gave myself more time to be alone. I realised that when I walked (as opposed to ran or cycled), I was slower and moved more rhythmically. I found it easier to reconnect with the inner me and experienced a *tremendous sense of peace as I found myself more in tune with the natural environment around me.*

I guess one of the biggest revelations that came to me at that time was that I had been living a lie my entire life, kidding myself about what was right and what was wrong, what was relevant or irrelevant. Walking in the big outdoors, on my own, gave me the time and space to meet myself, to think honestly and reflect on me, who I was, and what I wanted to be. It was while out walking that I stumbled upon, and later came to perfect, the most treasured of skills - the art of lack of self-judgement.

And that's what still happens every time I go out walking. I allow myself the time to reflect without judgement. I allow no room for blame, guilt, worries or concerns, and, in so doing, I am able to heal myself. Doing it outdoors in the natural world is a brilliant cure-all, not just for me, for everyone. I can't heal myself in a crowded and noisy gym where I find no inner peace. I can't heal myself by filling time with the poison on TV or joyless, house cleaning. I find it really difficult to heal myself when walking and chatting with other people because, while it is enjoyable, there's seldom opportunity for reflection. When I need to allow myself time and space to reflect without self-judgement and to heal, I need to be by myself in nature.

Around the same time that my healing got underway, it occurred to me that, up until that time on the rock, there was perhaps another reason why I had always been angry. Perhaps it had been necessary in order for me to survive. A self-defence mechanism as it were. And, having made it through the rock experience, I was now discovering that I didn't need to be angry anymore. Now that was an amazing revelation.

.../...

Sunrises and Sunsets

During my younger years, I loved to watch the burning red-orange fire of the sun as it silently and grandly crashed through the earth's surface somewhere out there over the distant horizon. Nowadays, I favour the elegant and graceful, serene and regal rising of the reborn sun each morning at dawn.

I often wonder why. Was it because when I was young and angry, the setting of the sun symbolised the end of yet another day of pain? Was it my metaphor for temporary closure on yet more anger, hurt and suffering? While I was struggling to figure out what the point of living was anyway, did sunset just represent ending?

Or is it simply because I have more peace within myself now? Nowadays, I relish each day that breaks and welcome the opportunity the universe presents to me to live life to the full and truly embrace feeling alive. Now that I am happier within myself and my world, does the sunrise remind me that my cup brimmeth over?

Or am I just getting older and more grateful to see another sunrise because I'm no spring chicken and time is starting to run out? Does another sunrise remind me to sort out my internal conflicts, find out who I am and what I'm supposed to be doing in this world before it's too late and I die without answers?

Perhaps all I really need to do is accept all the sunrises and sunsets as they happen, seeing them as part of a never-ending cycle inextricably linked to my life-force, containing all the beginnings and endings of my life. Perhaps sunrises and sunsets are best not questioned for they carry no answers. Or, perhaps the answer is simply too obvious: sunrise - awakening, sunset – sleeping. As with my own beginnings and endings, perhaps I should do no more than sit back and accept them, admire them even, but always revere them.

I must have dozed off for a short while because suddenly I jumped with a start as I felt the intensity of the sun's heat searing the tip of my already burnt left ear. I got up and took a final look at the open valleys extending out behind the pilgrim statue. If I was going to get to Triacastela before nightfall, I needed to get a move on. I smiled to myself as I started to pick up the pace; at least it was a fast and easy downhill from here. I didn't need to look for the way-markers and so took the time to remember a little more about what had happened and what I had learned in my post-rock days.

…/…

When I eventually built up the courage to tell my friends the truth about what had been happening in that relationship, they didn't judge, they didn't condemn, they consoled. I was shocked at how naïve I had been, assuming they would have sided with my partner and joined in his way of thinking. I was instantly made aware that I had been fearful of their reactions for so long and apparently for no reason. And then I remembered that I hadn't been able to think clearly because I'd been brainwashed by his way of thinking. He had wanted me to believe that I screwed everything up when in fact my friends knew me better. They knew my faults, but also my strengths, and I had underestimated just how valuable that would have been if I had trusted them. Not easy at the time, I know, but a lesson to remember for the future. Nowadays, I know better. If anyone starts to even suggest that I'm a bad person or tries to catalogue a list of my shortcomings, I cut to the chase and walk away so both of us can enjoy a better life without the interim hassle!

And please don't get me wrong, I'm not kidding myself (nor anyone else for that matter) that my life hasn't continued to be a series of ups and downs since that time maybe fifteen or sixteen years ago now. Of course, there are still ups and downs in life but I've discovered that the ups and downs are smoother, not as high or as low, and I come back from them quicker, bounce back more easily, more calmly, and I don't hold on to them like I used to in the past. I don't hold on to the pain either. I release it as soon as I can and I do this out of self-respect because I know that I am worthy of being me and enjoying my life. I also know that it screws up my body leaving the stress to build up inside and so I adopt the 'better out than in' philosophy. I have the right to not suffer. I choose to not suffer and so I learned to let go of things so much faster.

I also learned that shutting down to die - and wanting to do it - was the result of a heightened sense of and extreme embodiment of fear. My fight-or-flight mechanism had broken down, given up, given in. I had been living life in such an extraordinarily, harmful and untenable state of fear that my body had finished by telling my mind that it couldn't cope and my mind, also wanting out, had obeyed and shut down.

Now I spend more time being me, discovering who I am, what I like, what I want to be, and how I manage my relationships with other people on equal terms so that there is always a two-way, give and take rapport and not one-sidedness. I also avoid getting caught up in other people's games, consciously trying to stay in charge of my own thoughts and emotions, not getting involved in the emotional dramas of others which just bring on unnecessary tension and yet more ups and downs in life. Doing these things - always being mindful - free me from fear.

Oh, and did I mention patience? Patience is also one of the messages I learned from the rock experience. Patience is the key to learning how to work through my anger. About a year after my rock event, I realised that the protective, bubble of bliss I'd been wrapped up in had somehow evaporated and so I was back to being human and having to deal with things myself. So I learned to recognise anger coming when I felt the steam rising in my mind. I only had to count to ten - and really focus on and visualise each number in turn - in order to cool it to the point where I really didn't give a damn about what had rattled me in the first place. And thereby hangs another good lesson. Most things that get us rattled are often so trivial that we can't remember them afterwards. And if we do remember, given a bit of time, a change in perspective and a calmer frame of mind, the so-called issue usually isn't worth revisiting and probably didn't really exist at all.

Ping!

Now that I am older, I believe I have come to know the difference between the rage of anger and the fire of truth. When I was younger, I instinctively knew my truth and was angry when I was prevented from expressing it and thus denied the inner peace that would come with it and which I so desperately sought. Anger was my manifested frustration at not being able to live my life in the way I believed it should be lived. It was my expression of resentment for being told to suppress my passion for living my version of events. Not being allowed to be me was unjust in my eyes.

Looking back on my life, I know that when someone was intentionally hurting either me or someone else, it would stoke up a fire of injustice in me so great that I would quite literally explode and do whatever I could to right the perceived wrong. Now, I see my truth clearly in every action and reaction that surrounded those so-called moments of injustice. Now, I accept that my truth is not the same as someone else's truth and the world is full of differing opinions.

A rising surge of anger is often no more than a mask disguising and defending a perceived abuse or slighted truth. The solution is not to stoke that anger into a seething rage but to calmly look at the apparent slight and see what needs to be done to resolve and dispel it. But the root of all anger comes from fear: the fear of being hurt. And the heat of all anger can be extinguished when we come to realise that there is no need to feel hurt. If we stem the tide of hurt, there is no need to feel fear.

She's always with me these days as my close friend and ally, Patience. Or at least, she is when I allow her to be. Sometimes I forget but she's always quick to come calling and remind me there's no point in avoiding her. Most things in life can be sorted with a little help from Patience. The world would be a better place if we all made better friends with her.

.../...

The next day I headed out early from Triacastela into a dark and silent morning. The Camino quickly turned into a stony, dirt path climbing through woodlands to the Alto Riocabo. There were no views opening out onto the surrounding landscape and, lacking distractions, I was left to focus on how uncomfortable and sticky I was, tramping along uphill in the half-light. The air was so heavy with dew that you could see it and my hair and face were soon damp and cold. It seemed to go on forever. When the woods did at last open up and give way to farmed fields, I was flooded with relief and, with renewed vigour, picked up my pace at the prospect of coffee and tortilla not far ahead.

By the time I reached Sarria, the dew of the early morning had transformed itself into a regular rainfall and I was once again glad for some respite when I ducked into a café on the outskirts of town for lunch stop number one. I'd done a rough twenty kilometres that morning and so, as usual, I found myself wondering whether I should stop or carry on. As ever, I determined not to stop when there still remained half a day's good walking time left. Noticing that the rainfall was as steady as ever, I sighed a little, donned my backpack and set out and up into the hills behind Sarria. The ascent was slow and gradual, largely winding alongside fields and country lanes. This would slow me down, I thought, but at least it was a tad warmer than it had been when I set out at first light.

At the small hamlet of Ferrerios I found an open café and was compelled to stop for lunch number two. For safety's sake, I nearly always stopped to take on food and liquid just in case there wasn't another opportunity for another twenty kilometres. I had sorely regretted the few times I hadn't. It was always a welcome stop, short and sweet, never

147

more than twenty minutes at most, before I set off again. Enough time to revive my feet and legs, wipe my runny nose and warm up my insides with coffee and food. After a short hike out of Ferrerios, the hills finally started to level out before dropping off steeply on the way down in to Portomarín.

Portomarín was a weird and magical place. Having tottered down some steep and tricky farm lanes for several kilometres and which played havoc with my knees, the Camino brought me quite abruptly to a road across which a bridge spanned the mighty Rio Miño. The river roared loudly and yet I couldn't see it flowing. In fact, it looked more like an ocean, perhaps only because I couldn't see an end to it. To my mind, it was as though this vast water body had been materialised in from some place elsewhere and didn't quite fit here: it was out of place after tramping through forests and along farming fields for so many kilometres. In order to gain entrance to Portomarín, you had to firstly walk across the bridge and then climb some very steep steps in order to pass under an arch that officially recognised the pilgrim's arrival into town. It was like entering a village scene from The Lord of the Rings trilogy. The day's walk had turned out to be much longer than usual after the mammoth, uphill climb out of Sarria and so I checked into the first *albergue* I came across, showered quickly and went to explore what else was going on in this quirky place before dusk fell.

It didn't take long. Portomarín was a busy place with plenty of *albergue* options, despite it not being particularly big, and I easily walked through it in very little time. There didn't appear to be anything going on at all and, since I wasn't yet hungry, I decided to walk back to the bridge and the bizarre archway to get a better feel for what it was supposed to be about. This also didn't take long. But strangely, by the time I reached the bridge, a thick fog had crept in veiling it completely and, to all intents and purposes, it looked like a cloud had simply dropped out of the sky. There hadn't been any signs of it just one hour earlier and now I couldn't see the bridge at all, let alone the bank on the other side. As I edged my way to what I thought would be the approximate, halfway point across the river, I stepped into an eerie and damp, grey half-light and, wondering why I was even bothering to grope my way along this bridge in a virtual blind state when I suffered vertigo at the best of times, I stopped to listen to the sounds of the river below. Not being able to see beyond the wall of fog, cloaked in its invasive and cloying misty wet, my sense of hearing was all I had left to depend on and even this seemed a little off kilter. As I stood on the bridge clutching the cold railing tightly lest I somehow fall or get sucked in, I listened to the water roaring beneath me. It felt as though it was drawing me in and so I held the railing tighter and, the more I listened, the more I heard. And in those moments I began to make out the ping! in the voice of the river and the meaning conveyed behind its gushing words.

.../...

My mother died six years ago and I was cool with that. I could see that one coming. My paternal grandmother died two years later at the grand old age of ninety-nine. I was cool with that too; it was in the natural order of things. My elder sister died two years later. This I also half expected and so I was also able to deal with that with much inner calm and serenity too. However, while I was getting good at accepting and dealing with death, my father wasn't.

When my mother died I was prepared for it and almost expecting it. Towards the end of her life she had come to accept me for the person I was, possibly with a little regret for having been so harsh on me in my younger years. I have reflected enough to know that she loved me in her way as best she could and that was that. As a child, I hadn't coped well with the manner in which she had raised me and, more than anything, I had yearned for some signs of love and acceptance that I could recognise. I was sorely disappointed and handled my distress and frustration as only a child could and would have dealt with it at the time: badly. In her latter years, we got on pretty well; in fact we saw more of each other than my two sisters did. I would even go so far as to say that we began to enjoy each other's company. But her body was starting to fail her in her early seventies and so when she died just after Christmas one year it wasn't a huge shock to me.

However, it broke my father's heart: my mother was all he'd ever known for fifty years of married life. With her brusquely gone (she unexpectedly died during a supposedly, standard stent procedure to unblock an artery), his life and his outlook on it changed radically. It was evident to me (from too well recognised first-hand experience) that he was living the classic symptoms of grief. After the initial shock of loss and denial came the guilt and grief and yet more guilt over the following year. The father I knew had never been vociferous but now he became more silent and more closed in on himself than ever, never sharing his thoughts, never unloading his burden. I believed he faced his first ever experience of loneliness and isolation.

We remaining family members left on the outside could see his pain as we silently looked in, locked out, mutely witnessing the man tumbling head first down his own black hole.

Silence, Stillness and Aloneness

There is no such thing as silence: wherever you are in this world there is always some noise, be it natural or man-made.

To my mind, the true sound of silence is the sound of nature because when we silence the mind we hear the healing song of nature singing back to us. In fact, it's always there singing to us in the whistle of the birds, the breeze whispering through the trees and the rasping scratch of the crickets. Nature's melody cries out to be heard. It feeds our senses and that feeding is how we receive our healing. In nature, sound and silence walk hand-in-hand, one cannot exist without the other. We are interdependent on this planet and therefore cannot live in vacuums of sight, sound, and feeling. And hence silencing the mind is surely the true definition of silence because it brings us back into communion with nature. A silent mind makes us understand and respect, see, touch, feel, hear, and taste our natural interdependent state. When we go out walking and looking for silence (perhaps to find inner peace), we open our eyes and ears and attune more to our surrounds. In achieving our own inner silence we open ourselves up, becoming more alive and harmonious with this natural world of which we are a living and breathing part.

Neither is there such a thing as absolute stillness for we are always forever breathing. By stillness then, I mean emptying ourselves of mind-clutter. Through walking, plodding out the kilometres step by step, establishing a rhythm and tuning our breath to that rhythm, we can, through space and time, find ourselves emptying our minds of daily trivia and begin to feel some growing inner stillness.

And when we find ourselves in that place of inner stillness with outer movement, as we hear the footfall we also hear the breath, the in and the out, the rhythmic movement of holding our space in the universe while being grounded stable and steady on the earth. It is at this time we can let go of all fears, all worries, all concerns - the truly insignificant minutia - because we can relax as we sink into knowing we are individually no more than a tiny part of a much, bigger picture.

And it is at these times of inner stillness that we realise that we are alone but not lonely. When we can accept the quiet within ourselves, and the peace and harmony that come with that inner quiet, then we realise we no longer have to fear being lonely. Being at peace and at one with oneself and enjoying one's own company then become the most beautiful of experiences.

As we relax, we can enjoy just being, we breathe more deeply, and we free ourselves up to becoming joyful and see with fresh eyes the beauty in every little thing around us.

It is in this state of inner stillness and outer motion, harmony and oneness with the world, that we experience the miracle of being able to pick up a bird sat in the middle of the road and put it safely on the wayside because it allows us to; it has no fear because it knows we are at one with ourselves, the world and therefore with it. It is at times such as these that we can walk through a forest and a wild boar or a deer simply stares at us without running or charging or a butterfly alights on our arm, seemingly content to enjoy sharing with us our journey into peace.

It is my belief that each of us is here on earth to experience our own sense of self in this lifetime. Walking in company, while enjoyable, will have others tell us their experience and share their thoughts but that doesn't necessarily help us to find our own true self. We have to journey alone to find that. Walking alone allows us the time and space so that we may arrive at a deeper understanding of ourselves or learn something new about our true essence. Being alone sometimes is a necessary part of living in order to learn. It helps us therefore learn how to live.

At the grand old age of ninety-eight, my father's mother broke her hip and so moved down from Yorkshire to Cornwall to live with him. He suddenly seemed to have a renewed sense of purpose and companionship. He had hated the silence of his house filled with so much empty space during his year alone after my mother had died. His mother, my paternal grandmother, going to live with him therefore soon helped to fill up his time and space again.

Nonetheless, once the initial joy at having company in his house had waned, things changed dramatically. My grandmother soon wore him down because she was extremely limiting in terms of mobility and mental stimulation: the fact that she was near blind didn't help either. She was heavily dependant on my father and, while he was a dedicated son, at the age of seventy-seven, becoming a primary carer was too much. However, fate stepped in and my grandmother didn't last a year before she developed throat cancer and died unaware and peacefully just three months after the diagnosis.

Alone in his home once again, my father re-found his sense of humour and this time seemed to relish the freedom. He went to the USA to see my younger sister and would come to France twice a year to see my husband and me.

.../...

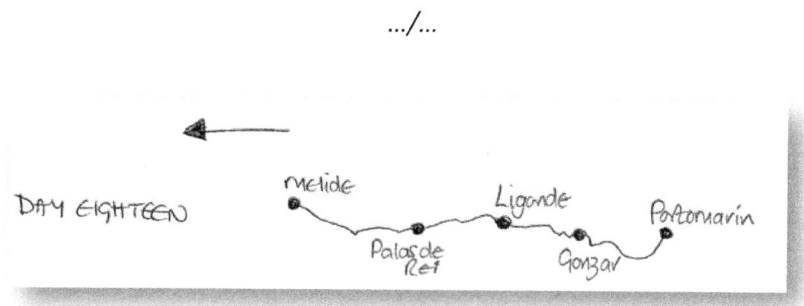

Early the next morning, I left Portomarín shrouded in the thick fog that had crept in to blanket the night skies the previous evening. That was eerie. I couldn't get over the feeling that the water hadn't finished with me, that it wanted to say more, and heavy precipitation followed close on my heels as I climbed, staying with me for the next eight kilometres until I finally shook it in Gonzar where the sun won the day bursting forth, evaporating the fog, forcing it to dissipate into the air. The rest of the morning's walk took me to Palas de Rei and, relishing the warmth of the sun now that my burnt ear had healed, I decided to stop longer than usual for lunch break number one so that I could visit a Pulpería and savour one of Galicia's favourite specialities, squid.

It was delicious. I loved the squid and the glass of crisp, white wine I had with it. Sat out on the terrace, backpack-free and basking in the warm sun, savouring my calming and fulfilling inner peace, I could have stayed there all afternoon. But some things are not meant to last. A little expresso later, I sighed and donned my backpack, looking forward now to a gentle afternoon of walking to Melide or thereabouts.

.../...

My father appeared to be doing better. But then my elder sister cocktailed out of life.

I'd flown over to Cornwall the week before Christmas to collect my father and bring him back to our house in France for the festive period. It was to be a big affair with my husband's family all present and my father was looking forward to the first good Christmas since my mother had died. However, the day we got back to my house, my niece rang to say her mother was dead. She'd been unable to reach her mum by phone for several days and so she'd reported her mother's drunken and depressive state to the police. They consequently broke in to her house and found her dead on the floor. My father's Christmas (and everyone else's) was, once again, not a good one.

Paraphrasing the coroner, he concluded that my sister's body had simply packed in after such a long period of alcohol and drug abuse. Needless to say, my eldest sister had not been a happy person. My earliest memories of her are marked by her fear of life, her lack of self-confidence, self-worth, and self-love. Pretty much like me really, but we had dealt with it in vastly different ways. She also had plenty of anger within her but reserved it exclusively for family members because she was too timid to assert herself with anyone else. The only two occasions I ever saw her looking really happy were her wedding day and when she gave birth to her daughter.

But my sister couldn't and wouldn't talk to anyone. We all saw her struggling with her own mental health issues and yet she would not accept nor seek help. A family trait of stubbornness ran through us all but there was also the unspoken expectation that we should not share our problems with others because it simply wasn't appropriate. It wasn't the done thing. Not surprisingly, everyone was ultimately locked out of her life (including her daughter in the end) and we continued to witness the devastation from a distance. She eventually managed to cocktail herself out of her living hell through a combination of prescription drugs and alcohol before she reached the age of fifty. It was possibly one of the saddest things I have ever lived through because I know first-hand what it's like to feel buried alive, blindfolded and inwardly screaming, from the darkest depths of a black hole of oblivion, where all there appears to be left to seek from life is numbing painlessness.

I don't hold myself responsible for her death. I also know what it's like to turn away from help when it's offered. But I do still wish there could have been another way for her to be happy in life. Fate may be what it is but to watch someone suffering from a similar problem to that which I had, and not be able to help, is an extremely painful and heart-rendering experience. My heart burned with the personal knowing of a similar suffering while my head screamed NO!!!! For a long time, it was like watching a Clockwork Orange-esque horror scene where I was forced to witness my sister torture herself – like a replayed variation of my own screwed-up and struggle-some misery with life - while my hands were bound and my voice muted.

But, at the end of the day, a simple truth remains. We, each of us, have to find it within ourselves to want to make a change if we don't like the life we have. No-one else can do it for us.

.../...

The Camino ran fairly close to the side of the road from Gonzar onwards and so for me it was not one of the most memorable or pleasant parts. Even in winter, when you'd expect the traffic flow to be vastly reduced, both the volume and the noise of the passing traffic felt fast and frenzied and disturbed both my inner and outer peace. My thoughts became as jumbled and chaotic as the traffic: I can't hear the bird song with that racket! Was that car heading straight towards me? Where have all the squirrels gone? How fast was that? Maniac! God only knows how much worse the volume of traffic got in summer. It probably wasn't that bad in fairness but there was a huge difference in potential for tranquil moments between the woodland and the roadside parts of the Camino. This section was loud and hectic and I was glad to rush through it as fast as I was able.

I arrived in Melide later than intended after that wonderfully, slow lunch in the sun at Palas de Rei and checked into a small *hostal* in the centre of town so I could relish a rare and glorious bath and make the most of washing my clothes in it afterwards. A standard Camino trick. Funny, I thought, at home I would never have a bath. I didn't like them and always opted for a shower. But, after another gruelling and dirty day of forty kilometres worth of footfall, bathing in warm water on the odd occasion that I did, unsurprisingly did much to revitalise me and gave me an instant feel-good factor. With the *hostal* TV dribbling on in Spanish in the background, I began to feel dozy and so closed my eyes, slid further down into the bath, and imagined pulling my snug, warm water blanket up closer around my neck.

.../...

Chapter Twelve: Re-Wiring

"Change the way you look at things and the things you look at change." Dr Wayne Dyer

Three close deaths in six years. Three denied opportunities to grieve and to heal. And these were just the deaths of his human family. My father's two faithful dogs also died of old age within this same timeframe not to mention some of his regular, golfing buddies. I guess the death of a daughter was the icing on the cake for him though. This one left him at an all-time low and, being the silent Yorkshire man that he was, he went further down a black hole into himself and said nothing.

Within a year of my sister's death, my father sold up and bought a house in the village next to ours in France. It certainly changed our lives as we spent a lot of time helping him with much needed DIY and the transformation of a neglected house. Coupling this with maintaining our own monster of an ancient house and our holiday flats, time seemed to eek away quicker than ever. My husband and I were often at our wits' end trying to establish a new way of living that now included my father, without ever really knowing what he wanted because he never spoke up.

Nevertheless, my father did pour himself (aching or numb?) heart and (damaged or denied?) soul into the renovation of his house and the landscaping of the gardens. His only love and passion still remains improving the gardens while, as far as everything else is concerned, he likes to portray the image that he's doing OK and getting along just fine.

But, dad, we can all see the obvious and painful scars etched on your weary forehead. And it's really hard to watch yet another sad and silent family movie. And, at the same time, all I really want to ask is: why is it that everyone in our family is too big to admit it when they need help?

Perhaps none of us is really aware that we need help until we've well and truly fallen down the black hole of our own making. Perhaps the real question should be: at what point is it too late to want to seek help? Perhaps there are some of us who genuinely don't want any help at all.

.../...

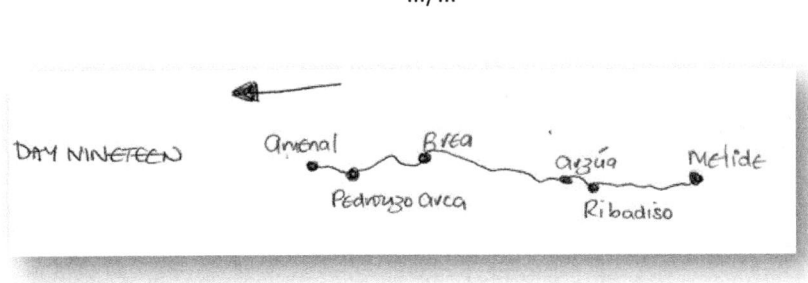

I set out early from Melide the next day with a skip in my step. The closer I got to Santiago, the springier I felt. The end was in sight. Slow down, I thought, it's not a race. I was starting to feel elated before I'd even got to the finish line. But the weather had changed and the base temperature was now much higher than it had been in the previous weeks: spring was definitely here and it was here to stay. It was possibly this that had me skipping my way through a day's worth of small villages and woods, over bridges and across streams, under bypasses and over roads, up and down hills, ever following the Camino, never straying far for food and drink, with Dorothy not far from my thoughts as I continued to follow my yellow, brick road. Yellow, brick road? I wonder why this had come back to mind. I hadn't given it much of a thought since the days spent on the Meseta. I casually visualised meeting the Wizard of Oz upon my arrival in the Emerald City of Santiago. I could even picture me clicking the heels of my battered boots together as I wistfully chanted, 'there's no place like home'. I ambled on until mid-afternoon admiring the trees and the woods, the small and quiet farming communities I passed through, and occasionally puzzling over the relevance and re-emergence of my mystical, yellow, brick road.

.../...

Had my father also been living through his own Clockwork Orange experience? Was he still dwelling in his private nightmare?

Of course he had and, to some extent, he still was. After the death of my elder sister, my father's personality had transformed radically so that I hardly recognised the man. He was often irritable, sullen or angry. I bit my tongue and retired into the shadows, silently observing, never bringing up the painful topics that needed to be addressed in order to heal, knowing from experience it would be futile. Patience told me to sit back and wait and see how things would surely unfold. 'This is something I am big enough to handle' I would tell myself and so I had to be patient, for my father's sake, until I understood the real issue at work. At times, it was really hard until it finally dawned on me what was happening.

He was still in shock.

I think the trauma my father lived through over that six-year period in which three key women in his life died was too much to deal with on his own, particularly at his stage of life. He was old-school and believed it was right and proper to keep a stiff upper lip. And yet, in choosing to say nothing, my father had been shutting himself off from people, life and living. For a formerly cheerful and care-free man, his mood now reflected his new outlook: dark and cloudy with no cheerful prospects worth looking forward to.

He hasn't stayed that way though. He still doesn't talk about anything painful but his devotion to the constant development and improvement of his garden has brought him to a quasi-peaceful state where he is certainly calmer and undoubtedly happier than when he first moved to France. The whole process has aged him and perhaps that is also why he is now calmer: age eventually catches up with us all, bringing us kicking and screaming or gracefully acquiescent into the next stage of our lives.

While this was going on, my life transformed beyond all recognition and that hurt a lot for a while as I initially tried to resist the inevitable changes. The reason I mention this is that, after all the healing I've received through self-reflection and years of walking and self-discovery, I realise that we never stop getting challenged in life by events and people. For me and my husband, a new tension had come into our hitherto quiet and peaceful existence and, trying to find a new life balance with my father so that it worked for everyone, had at times been physically and mentally demanding. Undoubtedly, it was just as stressful for my father too, but since he didn't talk about painful things, it took us a whole lot of guessing and a goodly while to figure things out. But, with a little patience and graceful acceptance from all three of us, things are now functioning well and we have found a comfortable equilibrium that seems to work for us all.

I guess I instinctively know now that when I was younger, with all the emotional ups and downs, the turmoil and the anger I had, I would have dealt with this situation far differently and it would have been disastrous. It still saddens me when I see people I know (and those I don't) keep painful things so close to their chest because it keeps them suffering when they don't have to. Funny how we all like to assume that no-one else could possibly know when bad things are happening to us in our lives. And yet, in truth, pain is so visibly etched on everyone's face when they are going through hell. In my father's case, I believe the surviving relationships he has in his life could still bring him more happiness and meaning if he would only be more open. A pain shared is a pain vastly reduced.

Choices, choices. We all have them and we would do well to remember that we have the right to change our minds and make new ones at any time without fearing the judgement of others.

Ageing with Grace

Many people fear getting older. Some fight it trying to stay, what I would call, super-fit in a forlorn attempt to scare off the ageing process. All they are really doing is idolising the body, seeing this as the benchmark for youthfulness. And at the other end of the spectrum perhaps are those who can't be bothered with exercise, the obese couch potatoes, who either don't care at all or may even rely on the inadequate, technological attempts of cosmetic surgery to keep them looking younger. Then again, there are those who are fierce exercisers because they lead stressful lives. They believe that raw strength is the only measurable yardstick and that a tough workout to beat the stress out of the body is the only code by which to live.

It came to me about five years ago that this is all wrong. Life is about finding a more harmonious balance of mind, body and soul. I am not arguing that we should not run marathons or stay fit and strong, but not listening to our body, mind and soul balance and ignoring the fact we are all ageing isn't a solution either. Looking after both our inner and outer landscapes is what brings lasting peace and helps us to bodily live and breathe better. We have to recognise when we are simply punishing ourselves and learn to stop it. Instead, we should focus on doing what genuinely suits us best.

If there is one thing that I've learned by completing the Camino twice, it is that my body no longer wants to walk between thirty-five and forty kilometres a day. I think I've pushed myself hard all my life, forever trying to do bigger and better. Now I recognise that I've been competing with no more than a ghost, an image of what I thought I should look like and how I should be. In later years, I hadn't been afraid to push myself hard because I was no longer afraid to die. On the contrary, I was now thirsty for life and hungry to express being me. However, sometimes to my own detriment, I have learned that some bad habits are hard to lay to rest. But the second Camino brought the message back home loud and clear: Be gentle on myself! Show myself some more respect! Start ageing with grace!

To my mind, we need to work with the ageing process - and thus our inevitable death - not against them by denial. It must be physically, spiritually and emotionally draining trying to avoid ageing and death. In order to work in harmony with the ageing process when walking, we should be mindful of how we feel with every step we take and, if we get a pain in the knee or ache in the shin or the foot, we should take it as a call to ease up and not push so hard. Why? Because we all know that what we resist, persists. Walking then can help remind us not to push too hard in life because the pushing often makes things more difficult. Walking helps us to stay fit and flexible so that we can glide into the future without being hit by the cold, sharp shock of reality when we wake up one day realising we can't run those marathons any more or we can't lift those weights like before and we are all going to die anyway.

Walking for relaxation, for pleasure, for reconnecting with nature, to find answers to questions which emerge, get answered and then disappear, helps put us at rest. Walking allows us to be at ease and at peace, within ourselves and our environment, to the point where we become accepting and at one with it all. And when we find this acceptance and oneness, we become fearless, we no longer have worries or fears and so start to relax and enjoy life. Walking is stress-less and natural and keeps us fit, physically, mentally and emotionally. I often like to think of myself as feeding my personal holy trinity while out walking since each step brings me into a better balance of mind, body, and soul. I certainly give no time to worrying about the prospect of getting older with every step I take towards my future and inevitable death.

I may be saying this backwards but I don't want to run away or hide from getting older. I don't want to fear ageing or death because they are going to happen regardless of what I do. I want to face them therefore with grace and for me that means staying fit, healthy, flexible and open-minded. And so while walking helps me to look after my body, I practise yoga to keep me supple and I meditate to keep my mind open and to help me stay grounded in the present moment and unstressed.

To find grace, everyone needs to find their personal 'thing' that brings them lasting peace, harmony and balance. I shall continue to enjoy whatever I am doing while I still can but, walking to find a better balance in my personal holy trinity of mind, body and soul union, now that's what I call ageing with grace.

Incidentally, one of my persistent thoughts about my family life issues is: Wow! There seem to be so many recurring themes, not just within one family member over a single lifetime, but up and down through the ages and between siblings. Wow! Why can't we ever talk about real and meaningful stuff? Why can't we share things? Why do we all think that we have to suffer? And alone in silence? What are we so afraid to face that makes us too scared to admit it when we've screwed up? Are we all so screwed up? Evidently so.

But my inherently defiant nature has me thinking and feeling a little differently now. I want to buck the trend. I want to be different. I want to react differently and I don't want to follow the family trend of suffering in miserable silence. I don't even want to be normal. I want to be me and to be allowed to be me. Me now is a happy person, loving a life free of fear. I want freedom and I'm in love with life!

We'll see where this takes us.

.../...

After having got stuck behind what appeared to be a mobile, thorn hedge of school children (a dense forest of least several coachloads) advancing loudly towards Pedrouzo, I carefully consulted the map and determined to detour a little and head towards Amenal instead. I'd spent several hours following these kids already and didn't look forward to the thought of doing the same again the next morning, let alone sharing an *albergue* with them overnight. I'd already spent a good few hours that day walking through some gloriously sun-kissed and (surely?) peaceful countryside that had been uncaringly and unconsciously peppered with high-pitched shrieks and giggles that quite literally smacked in the face of the beauty of the landscape. I had sorely missed my peace and solitude and was trying hard to resist the urge to feel affronted.

But in Amenal that night I faced another struggle. It was to be my last night on the Camino and I slept badly I think for several reasons. My feet and ankles hurt enormously, not because of blisters, but rather two swollen ankles and I believe a damaged nerve in my right foot. My toes felt strangely alien and distant. My shins ached and their constant nagging kept me awake for hours, making me recall that I had limped quite a bit over these past two days. I had also stopped for the night in a village or hamlet that didn't have an *albergue*. Instead, I was lodged in an expensive hotel that was cold because the heating wasn't working. I was frozen and struggled to sleep, weighed down as I was in as many layers of clothes I was able to don, buried under a heavy blanket that I'd found in the bottom of a cupboard.

It didn't get me down though. After almost three weeks of walking in initially cold and wet conditions and latterly hot sun, tormented by a miserable cold that was only just now showing signs of easing up, I was eager and excited at the prospect of arriving in Santiago the next morning and this had kept driving me on, regardless of the painful hobbling I had endured over the last two days. I knew also that the train journey from Santiago to Barcelona and up into France would give me fourteen hours with which to catch up on some sorely, missed sleep.

I'd purposely chosen to stop the night here this time around for three reasons. Firstly to avoid getting caught up with walking with the rowdy, school kids in the morning, the thought of which made me shiver. Secondly, the last time I passed through here in the searing heat, some people I'd met en route stayed the night there and I recalled how wonderful it looked in the sunshine as they laughed and downed their cold beers, elated to have successfully completed yet another day on the

Camino with no new blisters to work on. I had wanted some of that sun and beer this time around. But it hadn't happened. Dark clouds that were both thick and low had set in keeping the chill close to the ground. Nevertheless, staying at this place left me just seventeen kilometres to complete the next morning into Santiago. That was the third reason. The last time I'd done the Camino, I'd left the last ten kilometres to finish the next day and I'd struggled to find an *albergue* open and offering food, even though I was on the very outskirts of Santiago. It had beggared belief. This time, there would be no rush to leave and so, when the next morning arrived, despite my eagerness to get to Santiago, I forced myself to stay in bed a little longer until I eventually succumbed to my growing hunger and went in search of breakfast. I made sure to eat heartily before setting out on my last day of the Camino.

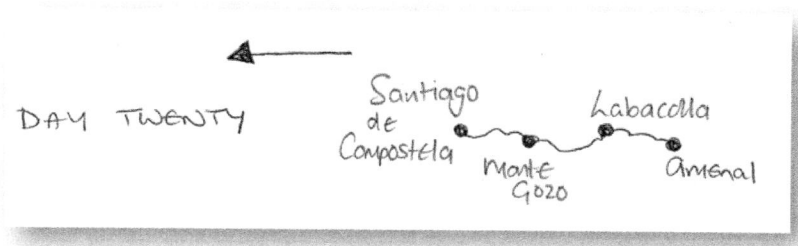

I remember well how cold it was that morning as I stepped out into a beautifully clear and blue-skied day and wondered, not for the first time, why on earth I was doing this in March. Ah yes, fewer walkers, less noise, more head space. I walked on. Leaving Amenal, the Camino initially climbed through dark woodland and it felt as though I was walking back in time into the dark of nightfall until I finally emerged into an sunny, open clearing which lead on and into the tentacles of concrete, suburban sprawl near Santiago airport.

But, as I reached the airport in the post-dawn hours of the day, the same thing happened to me this time as it did the last: I found myself crying. Not tears of sadness or tears of joy. Tears of relief perhaps resulting from a sudden, corporeal awareness of the extraordinary amount of endurance I had asked my body to muster up in order to do the Camino – once again - in just twenty-one days. Having the tenacity to walk 780 kilometres, to my mind, also required dogged patience and so perhaps all these things had been present flowing through my mind at some level or another on those last Camino stretches on both occasions.

I found myself walking alone as usual but with a periodic build-up and release of tears as I thought about this or that incident, this or that learning curve, this or that recollection that I'd had along the way. At the same time, I found I was laughing and crying at the hidden woodpeckers' frantic tapping and the whisper of the wind tickling the leaves in the trees. I smiled and cried at the crunch of cold pebbles under my freshly glued (oh yes, every night!) boots, and the beautiful lacework the spiders and a bit of hard frost had delicately woven through the grass and dandelions lining the Camino as it wove its way through the last of the woods. I shuddered with cold and cried at the sound of the icy waters of the pregnant brook racing by under footbridges and the surge of foggy chill that arose from the waters enveloping me as I crossed over them. Everything was glorious, magnificent, cold and yet coming to an end. Ping!

That was it! My journey was ending. That's why I was crying.

.../...

Chapter Thirteen: Finding Peace

Reading Dante's Divine Comedy was one of the best things that could have ever happened to me.

It has dawned on me that, so far in this book, I have recounted some of the most memorable encounters and events that I weathered through while out walking the Camino. I have shared with you some of the positive and negative reflections I made on all manner of things that affect our daily lives and levels of peace and happiness. In doing these two things, I have also related (and tried to make sense of) the most traumatic aspects of my life. What I haven't yet done is redress the balance of the latter and tell you about a big positive in my life such as meeting my husband. Why should I, you may ask? Because my life is not just a series of unhappy events. I met and married another man who I am still married to after thirteen years. And to this date, we are able to laugh and smile and are the best of friends. Does this then mean that this is the end of the dramas in my life?

In my last job in England, I had to drive up to Head Office for a regional managers' meeting once a quarter. It meant staying two nights in a hotel and usually, because of the traffic, I tried to get there earlier rather than later so I could chill, read and relax rather than sit in a traffic jam on the M1. On this particular occasion, I had found the hotel, showered and done my emails, and it was still too early to meet the other managers for dinner. At a bit of a loss and wondering what to do next, I impulsively picked up my book and headed downstairs to the bar for a glass of wine.

It was Friday night and people were starting to drop in for a quick drink after work, catching up with friends and colleagues before they went

167

home for the weekend. Rather than read my book, I found myself people-watching, as I usually ended up doing, until I recognised one man in particular enter the bar and I quickly ducked my head down into Dante's Inferno. I don't know why I did that but less than a minute later the man was stood in front of me saying 'hi'. No escaping it now, I thought. And so he bought a drink and we sat together and we talked.

I had known Bob as a colleague for about four years and, barring the occasional 'hi' once a quarter at work, we had never really spoken. But I knew he had recently lost his wife and, in offering my condolences, a conversation ensued about death, loss and grief that neither of us had ever experienced before. He needed the discussion and I realised that, after all that had happened in my life, I did as well. At a time when it was still taboo for many to talk openly about these issues, we found peace and understanding, acceptance and calmness. This was my first ever experience of meeting another human being and talking in complete, unabashed honesty. What a revelation and what an immense relief!

Over the next year, our friendship grew and, over time, the themes of our conversations expanded. Our chats always involved coming together, meeting, talking passionately and in complete honesty with each other. From the start, we bared open our souls and shared the shameless truth about our lives, our past experiences, as though we'd known each other for centuries. It was such an incredibly, refreshing experience I would go so far as to say that it felt like a soul-deep cleansing. It was beautiful. It set the stage for a huge amount of trust to develop between us over the years and because of that we became and remain the deepest and best of friends. And all because we respected each other and ourselves enough to be honest from the start. How amazingly simple is that? We were able to form a relationship on solid foundations because nothing was masked or loosely based on hidden half-truths that our egos had nudged forward in a vain attempt to make ourselves look better in the eyes of the other.

When I looked back on previous relationships, most of them were built on having my partner believe one thing or another about me that I thought would put me in a better light. Sometimes this was a conscious move, most times it wasn't. But either way, I came to realise that it was self-delusional because other people inevitably see us for what we really are anyway and the truth always outs in the end. An already failing relationship will undoubtedly collapse when the truth is partial or non-existent. These days, my marriage is proving to be a special and lasting experience because we voiced our truth first and, in doing that, we discovered how we could work out the lasting relationship that we still enjoy together today.

But that's not all of it. I believe a successful relationship must allow you to feel safe and yet give you the space and freedom in order to let you be the person you are meant to be. Your partner then has to support you in this, just as you must support your partner. Acceptance, not judgement, is key, as are patience and forgiveness. From practicing and enjoying these things, we can breathe and relax, laugh, love and be happy, both together and separately, comfortable with who and what we are in life, independently and in sharing one together. Finally I have come to understand that this is what a perfect home means for me.

My husband gives me all this and I say to him now, thank you. Thank you for showing me what home looks like and what it truly means. Thank you for helping me to set myself free. You enable me to both define my world and help me keep re-creating it to suit the ever-evolving me. Our relationship is expansive allowing everything we do to be based in, and stem from, a position of love not fear. Freedom is the absence of fear. Freedom is thus love. Being love, feeling it and sharing it, is living life. There should be no room in anyone's life for fear.

The reason for adding this positive is because it is something that would not have been possible if I had not learned about myself, making my self-discoveries while out walking. And so I say thank you to me too!

I have arrived. I am home.

.../...

Happiness, Inner Peace and Love

Since I was very young, all I ever remember wanting from life was to be happy. For many years, I dreamt of reaching this ultimate state of being, my nirvana; but, at the same time, I thought I didn't deserve to be happy and so it was in effect an unreachable dream. And then, one day, I woke up. I realised that the one thing that stopped me from achieving happiness was the mere act of always wanting it. While I was forever in a state of *wanting* happiness, it was always a future event that hadn't happened and wasn't happening. As such, I could never have it, it was unobtainable, and so the trick was to turn things around by just *being* happy.

Nowadays, for me, happiness can be found in admiring a solitary dewdrop on a leaf while out on an early, morning walk. The raw beauty of it makes me smile on the outside and on the inside. Watching a dragonfly zip back and forth in all its wondrous colours and prehistoric shape makes me smile on both the inside and the outside too. In fact, watching anything moving or living in its natural, unfettered state makes me feel happy.

It hit me in a marvellous ping! moment that happiness is a state of mind as well as a state of being. It is a state of accepting what is and not denying what is or even what isn't. Happiness is being content with who and what I am, not refuting my shortfalls, accepting them with grace. Moreover, it is about knowing what my strengths are, accepting, acquiescing, knowing that I do indeed have strengths and that I should use them with grace to help myself and others equally.

To my mind, being happy can help bring about inner peace and, conversely, finding inner peace can bring about happiness. Accepting myself as I am, others as they are, and the world the way it is, letting things just be, helps me to achieve both inner peace and happiness. In so doing, I realise that happiness comes when we find ourselves to be kind and loving to ourselves, to others, and to everything around us in the world. I believe the two are inextricably linked. You cannot be happy without being loving and not loving without being happy. I've come a long way since the days when I used to believe that I didn't deserve to be loved or wasn't able to love. Now I know that I am, not only deserving of love, I am loved and I am love.

Each time I walk, it helps me to open my eyes (and my awareness) to my outer world and I become grateful for every living thing that I see, smell, hear, or walk past. I find myself mindful of all that is around me at that moment in time and I am thankful for it. This state of gratitude for my outer world then helps me to accept my inner world with more grace. As I walk in this state of happy peace, I begin to rediscover myself as though I am walking back to myself, and it helps me to love myself a little bit more. Love, I've discovered, is one of the most powerful tools for self-healing and, without walking, I doubt I would have come to realise this for a very long time, if at all. By love, I don't mean the physical act of love-making or needing to be loved by someone else to feel worthwhile as a human being. I made this mistake for most of my life. Now I know I don't *need* for anything. I don't need someone else's love in order to feel loving or loved. I don't need for something outside of myself in order to be a complete person.

The only way to feel complete is to be myself. To have unearthed an awareness of who and what I am, and to continue making new discoveries as I dig further within each and every day of my life, to be content with who I am, what I am and what I do, is a form of love: self-love. It's taken me many years to realise how desperately important this is, how fundamental, how critical, it is for each and every one of us to be able to show love for ourselves.

When I woke up on my forty-fifth birthday and realised I needed to go walking more than I ever had before, more frequently and for longer distances, in order to learn to have no fear in life, I did not know then that five years later I would devote the rest of my life to the constant and continual discovery of who I am with an ever, expanding notion of love for myself and for others.

Nowadays when I'm out walking and a butterfly comes to rest on my arm, not only do I know that I have found my place and space back within nature, that I've reconnected with the natural world, I know also that the butterfly would not be resting on me if I had not found my sense of inner peace, my love, my happiness. If I was at odds with myself, I would be out of sync with my surroundings too, and the butterfly or the wild boar, the deer or the eagle, would not venture anywhere near me. And sometimes, when they do stay away from me, it helps raise my awareness that I am not right in my skin and that something is out of kilter that needs righting in my mind, body, and soul balance. A rebalancing of love is usually what's required.

As I continue to age (and hopefully also grow and learn), I like to visualise myself not so much as walking away from fear but rather moving towards love. Moving towards love requires the absence of fear.

Happiness, peace and love. I am happy. I am loving. I am love. You cannot be happy without love. You cannot find freedom without love. Love is freedom. Love is found in the absence of fear.

What I haven't said before now is that, when I first came to spend time with and truly start getting to know Bob, he had already decided to take early retirement and head out to the south of France to spend the rest of his days reading and writing in relative peace as he was wont to do. You may have just guessed then that within a relatively short period of time the inevitable question arose: 'What was I going to do?'

Bob and I had spent a good few months simply enjoying each other's company and healing our wounds in the process. I hadn't given the future a second thought; I was too content with living in the here and now. But Bob's leaving date from work loomed closer and the stark reality came knocking on my front door one day as Bob told me he would be gone within a few months.

I inhaled deeply trying to keep calm as Bob's announcement coldly slipped into the fuggy numbness that had somehow crept into my head and was now cloying my brain. Was this yet another relationship ending in my life? Was possibly the best thing that had ever happened to me just walking out the door when we hadn't even really got started? Feeling head-dizzy and slightly nauseous, I began to shrink back into my former self as I watched the war-weary, dysfunctional, emotional patterns of the past start to re-emerge.

…/…

I found it strange to have to climb up and into Santiago. In my head, I was arriving at my destination and that meant it should be flat or, better yet, an easy downhill after one heck of a long, uphill journey within myself. So, to have to firstly climb up to the airport, and then up again some more to the campsite, threw me off balance. Yet more hard work, regardless of all I'd put in over the past few weeks; was nothing in life easy? But soon after the Monte Gozo, the Camino did start to descend quite rapidly into the city.

I crossed the bridge with tears still burning the corners of my eyes and I had the weird sensation that everyone driving towards me could see my tears and was wondering what had happened. I tried to dispel the thought but as I started to walk up the city streets heading for the *catedral*, it kept returning to me because now there were lots of people walking past, looking at me and moving on. It must be my walking staff, the backpack, the dirty clothes, I figured. That's what they were staring at. And, seeing that I was a crying pilgrim with a smile on my face? They were probably concerned at their own proximity to this walking weirdo.

Undaunted, I ambled along the modern, concrete slabs lining the streets of the new town. They soon transformed into cobbled paths as I reached and then traversed the old, historic town and, finally, after three weeks on foot, the end of the *Camino Francés* brought me right to the *catedral* in the Centro Histórico. The sun was now perched on high in a clear, blue sky and was trying its best to offset the cold chill of the wind. I stopped in the middle of the square and turned to face the *catedral*. I breathed deeply allowing myself this moment to assimilate my achievement, the journey: the beginning, the end, and everything that had happened in between. I felt full and rich as I stood and stared at the enormous *catedral* before me. Was this it? Was the Wizard from the Emerald City at the end of my yellow, brick road in there? I stood and stared hard at this magnificent building waiting to feel a bit of magic enter my veins. Nothing. I tried clicking the heels of my walking boots, just as Dorothy would have. Nothing. It left me cold. I had walked for three weeks, always heading to this very point, this culminating venue, surely I was supposed to feel something?

Ah, but hang on a minute... and I felt the buzz of a now familiar ping! This time it was a little warm and fuzzy, like an old friend tapping me on the shoulder, winking at me with a smile at the dawning of my comprehension. Of course, I knew where to find the Wizard! The Wizard was responsible for everything I had ever lived through - both good and bad - and who made me what I am today. The Wizard had always been there right from the start, the one person I should be most grateful to, and to whom I owed thanks for everything that had ever happened to me in my life.

If I had discovered anything while walking the Camino, it was that the Wizard was in me. I was my own Wizard. I was responsible for everything that ever happened and ever would happen to me. And then came another ping! which slot beautifully into place. 'There's no place like home.' Ah, I get it now. The journey was all about finding me, discovering me, knowing me, so that I could eventually come back home to me.

I have arrived. I am home.

.../...

I should have known better. I was a different person to who I was way back when I sat down on that rock to die. I had been re-wired so many times since then and knew myself better. I had more self-esteem than ever before and should not have so readily, so unconsciously, started to tumble head-first into a former, negative way of thinking.

Bob smiled at me and my worried look when he announced his imminent departure down to the south of France. And, in the very next breath, he asked me whether I would consider going too. 'What?' I'd replied, I hadn't given it a moment's thought. And his face creased kindly into a broad smile as he then said, 'Is there any reason why you can't or why you shouldn't?'

I thought about his question for two days and my mind just kept coming up blank. I had spent the past few years re-building myself, under my own steam, and was now starting to enjoy life and living and develop into the person who I was just beginning to find out I was meant to have always been. After two days, my head was still blank until it gradually dawned on me as to why. It was simple. Over the past few years I had created an entirely new existence for myself and built up a strong sense of self-worth within this latest, cocooning world of mine. Bob was now asking me to leave that safety net and try something else and part of me was terrified at the thought of leaving this recently found, blissful, safe haven.

And then my mind swam rapidly through to a new realisation. The safe haven was no more than an illusion just like anything else in life. From the moment Bob had walked in on Dante and me in the bar, my world had been changed and there was no going back. Life doesn't work like that; you can't go back. Nothing ever stays the same. Life is actually quite simple. The only way is forward. And as this new dawning came over me, I smiled for the first time in two days and rang Bob to say that the answer was a very obvious yes. Of course I would go with him to France. I couldn't think of one single reason why I shouldn't or couldn't.

Ah, but then I could really. Fear.

Fear would have been the only reason to prevent me from going and I am just so glad that I refused to entertain that old joker once again. I could have lost everything. But instead I gained everything and I learned that I truly never had anything to lose anyway.

Love and life. Love of life. Love of living and moving forward. Never fear.

.../...

I have arrived. I am home.

Having spent three weeks finding myself while walking the Camino, I had now reached the proverbial end of the line. I wondered if, with all the insights and new learning about myself, I had in some small way been reborn again or whether that only ever happens to anyone once in a lifetime. I guess I would have to live life some years more in order to find out. I spent a few minutes more taking in the enormity of the *catedral* in front of me and the magnitude of the Wizard within me before I slowly turned and headed off in search of the Pilgrim Office. I'd be coming back to explore the *catedral* later.

I hadn't felt drawn to enter a single church while walking the Camino, such had been my resolve to deny God and His church. Strange, some would say, since for most people the Camino is first and foremost a religious pilgrimage to be undertaken by those seeking to find a closer connection to God. To help them on their way, the path is quite literally littered with churches, shrines and cathedrals, the accepted places that were constructed to facilitate such divine communication. But for me, my church has always been and still remains the beauty of the great outdoors. I hadn't ever felt a need to enter a building to see the divine beauty in everything around me. Neither had I wanted anyone to preach to me about the need to show gratitude for God's beauteous and gracious bounty. Some things you just implicitly know yourself.

But now I was in a different place. Now my anger at this mammoth, religious institution that man had created was spent. No, better than that, it was extinguished, vanished, evaporated. Now I felt strong enough within myself to let it all go. It no longer mattered. There was quite simply no room or need for anger anymore and so, overflowing with an enormous sense of peace and serenity, I took the decision, there and then, to stop denying the existence of this giant body of collected belief and let it be.

We each of us, consciously or unconsciously, are forever seeking to discover our own truths and answers from our lifetime's personal experiences. The way in which we choose to experience our spiritual communications and connections is deeply personal and many, many thousands of people seek and receive solace from organised, religious institutions all over the world. I now accept that. Ping!

Upon reaching the *catedral* in Santiago after three weeks of walking the Camino, I finally came to resolve what was perhaps one of the biggest issues of my life. My attitude towards God had always been to treat Him as though He physically resided in a man-made church. In fact, in each and every church that was built in His name. Worse, that He displayed the same petty characteristics of a human being. Because I'd been disappointed by a handful of priests I'd met along my life journey, I'd effectively tarred the lot of them with the same brush and locked them up in their churches with their like-minded, mean God and thrown away the key. Nothing like being open-minded, eh, Joanne? Because I had also subconsciously sought to find someone to blame other than myself for every miserable and unpleasant thing that had ever happened to me throughout my life, I'd found it all too easy to blame the mystical and magical element called God for all my personal failings and short-comings. For too long, I had avoided looking within at where the real root of all my problems lay. For too long, I had avoided standing up, being courageous and honest with myself and taking a really good, close look at what I didn't like about me.

But now, finally, I had done it. I had stood up and faced myself. I had dared to stand before myself and I had braved my own judgement. I had tested myself. And I had come to learn that there was no need for judgement. In fact, there was absolutely nothing wrong with me and I categorically had nothing to atone for.

Furthermore, I had come to understand that the real God lies within. The whole point of God, my God, my Wizard, my own shining light, is what I am truly all about. It's what we are all about and it is the only thing that is important in life. Finding out who we are, discovering our own shining light within, and living up to being the best we can possibly conceive for ourselves. This, surely, is finding God.

I knew I had no apology to make to the Church or to God. Indeed, I would only have been apologising to myself. Instead, I congratulated myself and thanked myself for having the strength to walk the journey to find my true self. But, in the spirit of extending a tangible olive branch, I decided I would visit the *catedral* at midday and attend the pilgrims' mass. I knew now that I could visit a church and find both God and myself in there and within me.

…/…

In the Pilgrim Office, I meet the most extraordinary person of the whole journey.

I believe the Pilgrim Office is run by volunteers and, while I stand in the queue trying to collect myself together and stop crying as I'd begun to bubble over yet again, I look around and see a host of warm and friendly faces among those volunteers sat behind the long counter. At that time of the morning, the queue is quickly processed and so I step up to the counter and handover my credencial to the man sat behind. He smiles at me and attempts some questions in his best English. Together, with my best Spanish, we stumble and falter. I feel a little tearful again and, while trying to compose myself, out of the corner of my eye I become aware of a kindly, matronly figure surveying us, trying to assess the situation. I turn to look at her square in the eye and she evidently sees in me that I have come a long way: more than a mere journey on foot. The lady makes a decision and comes from around the counter and approaches me with her arms out-stretched. She falls short of me by the distance of a single step and looks at me now, questioningly. Ping! I know she is asking my permission and without faltering or stopping to think – having sought a recollection of one single moment such as this with my mother across my entire lifetime – I fall sobbing into her welcoming and motherly, open arms.

> *I have arrived*
> *I am home*
> *In the here*
> *In the now*
> *I am solid*
> *I am free*
> *In the ultimate*
> *I dwell*[4]

Thank you, Thich Nhat Hanh, for this wonderful enlightenment.

.../...

Walking gives me an outer space that allows me to detach myself enough from everything going on in my life so that I can find the calm, inner space from where I can reflect on life more clearly. Whether it's the Camino, a long trek or another pilgrimage, to me the point of the long walk is to allow the trail to enable me to reflect, to become aware, to make observations, to let go. And in doing this, each time I set myself freer than I could previously imagine. Freedom is expansive. And, free from fears of the past and the future, I find both inner peace and happiness.

---

[4] Thich Nhat Hanh

I am not kidding myself that it all ends there nor that I will never again experience ups and downs in my life. But, I know that I shall keep walking and keep making new discoveries about my personal truths for the rest of my life because this is precisely what life should be about. We change, we evolve, we become greater. But to do this, we have to be brave and go walk alone. Nobody else can discover us in place of ourselves.

.../...

Chapter Fourteen: The Never-Ending

My personal story of the Camino and me may have come to an end. But I realise now that there is no end. There is only evolution. The truth is never-ending, only ever-evolving.

Five years ago, I embarked upon a journey. No ordinary journey in the modern Western sense of the word, but a personal journey requiring physical and mental strength and, above all, a burning desire to search for the truth. I knew my personal challenge was to learn how to live life fearlessly. I discovered that this would also bring me the only two things I had always wanted from life: freedom and happiness. It turned out that I discovered many personal truths along the way.

As I set out on this journey of inner and outer exploration, I instinctively felt compelled to start an 'out-in-nature' diary, taking notes of what I saw and felt, and saving voice recordings of what came to mind each time I stepped out the front door into the green beyond. It was only later that my husband read part of the diary and, liking what he saw, decided to listen to some of the recordings and he became hooked. It was at my husband's suggestion that I did the Camino in March 2015 and, three years later, I did it again. While I was away walking the second time, my husband collated all of the above into a book and convinced me that millions of women were waiting to read this. Friend of a friend, Sarah, gave me the final, convincing nudge. I say thank you again to my husband and Sarah for pushing me to do this and for all the encouragement along the way. I also hope that my husband is right and that this book really does help motivate not just women – everyone - to go out and walk in this beautiful world that we've been blessed with, and start their own personal reconnection with nature.

Why? Because this is just a little of what I discovered.

Fear.

Fear is defined in the dictionary as being an unpleasant emotion caused by the threat of danger, pain, or harm. Suitable synonyms are: terror, fright, fearfulness, horror, alarm, panic, agitation, trepidation, dread, consternation, dismay, distress, anxiety, worry, angst, uneasiness, apprehension, nervousness, nerves, unrest, perturbation, foreboding, misgiving, doubt, suspicion. More informally: the creeps, the willies, the heebie-jeebies, the shakes, the collywobbles, jitteriness, twitchiness, butterflies (in the stomach), the screaming abdabs, or, in rhyming slang, the Joe Blakes.

As a verb, fear is defined as: to be afraid of someone or something, as likely to be dangerous, painful, or harmful. Suitable synonyms are: afraid of, be fearful of, be scared of, be apprehensive of, dread, live in fear of, be terrified of/by, tremble before, be anxious about, worry about, panic about, feel consternation about, have forebodings about, feel apprehensive about. More informally: have a phobia about, have a horror of, have a dread of, shudder at, take fright at.

Having fear means that one avoids doing something because one is: too afraid, too scared, too apprehensive, or dares not.

How dreadful. How restrictive is all that? It makes me feel quite ill just reading through the list. Now I understand why I woke up on my birthday knowing that I had to ditch this notion of fear: it's not just a notion. Fear can be physically and mentally debilitating. Fear has us begging for mercy, leaves us crawling on our knees and, all the while, is cruelly killing us from the inside out. Living in fear is possibly one of the worst things that we can do to ourselves and yet we all do it! Fear destroys the best in us, even though we know it's not good or healthy for the human body, mind or soul. But, thanks to my experiences, I now know why I prefer not to spend the rest of my life living in fear of myself or anything else.

Reciprocally, two antonyms for fear are calmness and confidence. Now that is precisely what walking has taught me about over the past few years: how to be calm and confident. I couldn't just *be* calm and confident, not with all that burning anger and fear inside of me. I had to learn how to become them which meant firstly, un-learning the anger, which meant secondly, un-learning the fear.

Anger comes from fear. I learned this while walking the Camino.

182

In my case, my body-shaking, white-fury anger emanated from a fear of being unloved, un-loveable, not worthy of being loved, not deserving enough to be loved. And through walking, I eventually learned that none of these things were true. As a child, I had not understood the other issues at play in my mother's life such as her relationship with my sisters and father. As a child, I felt that my mother was unable to give me what I needed in order to feel loved and worthy of love. I assumed it was because of me, my fault. It probably was. She presumably didn't have the time or the energy for me since I never slept. She was doing all she could to stay sane herself running the house, the marriage and three children single-handedly while my father went off to work or to play cricket. My sisters and I weren't the only ones who never saw him, my mother didn't either. All this in an era when things were not so convenient or as easy as the internet has made things today. I was also a very sensitive, hyperactive and thus hugely demanding child which just compounded my mother's problems. Today, I know that my mother could only ever show me love in the way in which she was able to give it - in her way, not my way. I probably just hadn't recognised it because it was not given in the way that I had wanted to receive it. That's one of the problems with being human right there.

My mother died about six years ago now but I have no regrets. We'd settled our differences beforehand and had come to a friendship with a mutual acceptance of each other's needs for space and identity. In a way, I'm a little sorry I couldn't have worked out the contents of this book before she died so that we could have talked about it. Talked about her. Her and me. But at the same time, I believe that everything happens for a reason and so her parting before I made my real discoveries was meant to be. As with the rest of our family, she was never a talker of real issues either and in all probability wouldn't have discussed it anyway. The fact remains that, through walking, I learned patience and, from this, I gained enough perspective to see things clearly and anew and, from this, my anger simply began to ebb away. I can now say, "I love you, mum. And I love me too." This is new.

About four years into this personal journey, I wanted to have a daily reminder of my goal. Jenny Joseph's poem 'Warning' ('When I am an old woman I shall wear purple, With a red hat that doesn't go, and doesn't suit me.') was starting to haunt me when I realised that I'd already been wearing purple for some years. So I got a tattoo instead – a dragonfly – a permanent and symbolic reminder to keep breaking through the illusion of entrapment in this life, to continue finding my freedom daily, to always walk and explore this beautiful world in which we live and for which we never seem to give enough gratitude. Appreciation of the outer world, I've learned, is key to appreciating the beauty of our inner world. If the outer world is a reflection of our inner selves, then surely we want to make it stunning, don't we? There is beauty to be found everywhere and in everything if we are willing to choose to see. If we want to change our lives, our world, then we need only change the way we see it. Change perspective and we can make anything truly great. This is one of the true magic gifts of life available to human beings.

I know now that walking helps me come back to myself, discover myself, re-find my true self and better understand me. In my case, there had, for too long, been a hidden me, a more real me, that went beyond the anger and lack of self-worth, and it was only walking that brought this to the fore. Walking helps me to understand my life experiences, my existence, the core of my very being, so that I can let go of the past and the future and be fully present in today. Walking helps me to release all those thoughts and emotions that are no more than unnecessary baggage. Everyone will have their issues, similar or not, that walking will likewise help to resolve.

This explains how I can truly send from the bottom of my heart a massive thank you to each and every one of the major players in my life story for all the good and bad experiences I have ever shared with them and which helped shape me into the person I am today. Thanks to the major challenges I have faced in my relationships with others, I have learned to refrain from judging, criticising or trying to control others. I let people be and expect them to let me be. I try to always speak my truth, show love and compassion towards others, and am conscious about enjoying life because I know that laughter, joy, and love are the real roots of deep healing. Knowing now that, what we see in life is a mirrored reflection of what we send out, it makes perfect sense to send out all the beauty we want to see coming back to us. We are the masters of our own creations and if we want to experience happiness, love and joy, then that's precisely what we need to give to others. Every experience for me these days I perceive as having a benefit, a lesson to learn, or just something sent to redirect me on to bigger and better things. When we are willing to change our perspectives in life, our lives change dramatically.

Let me also make it clear that I am not seeking perfection. I think everything is already perfect the way it is otherwise it wouldn't be like that, would it? That is why we should all learn to respect others, let them be themselves, not try to control or change them. We change ourselves when we want to and are ready to or not at all. It's a conscious or subconscious choice.

Depression, Addiction and the Earth

How it starts or where it begins is not the same for everyone. Whether there's a trigger called grief or stress, anxiety or low self-esteem, addiction or depression, or something entirely different, is not always known. But, ostensibly and quite suddenly, a fragment of your awareness comprehends that some tattered and broken remnants of the person you formerly used to recognise as yourself are sinking in a dark and desolate, bottomless abyss. Trying to find yourself can seem pointless because you don't know where you are and you no longer recognise the pieces that are left which once were you. You've lost yourself down there and you see no way out. You are cold and numb.

I know what it's like to be stuck in a place, unable to move for an interminable number of hours because the energy, the inclination, the awareness or even the simple reason to do so, just isn't there. I know

185

what it's like to have lost the 'exit' of your nightmare and not have the energy to look for it: trying to find a way out or to get 'unstuck' doesn't even feature on the radar.

I know how much of a struggle it can be to walk twenty paces let alone walk for twenty minutes. If your personal world has ever bottomed out, my message to you is simple. This is a good thing.

If you've hit the bottom and lost yourself, it's because you've lost the person that you no longer recognise or want to be. You've also lost the life that wasn't working for you and so now you have two options:

Give up, let go and try again in the next life (you have to believe in reincarnation for this to work). Or,

Recognise that something really, deep inside of you knows where you are and wants you - is urgently willing you - to find some ounce of courage to stand up yet again. Part of your consciousness is kicking and screaming at you to stop living the life that you hate so much. Part of you wants you to find out who you really are so that you can become all that you so totally want to be.

If you are reading this and feel stuck, stand up and take a single step. And then another. Count every step as a victory and personal achievement of some note. Every step forward is indeed a step forward and there is no race to get to the finish line. Remember that. There is no race because there is no finish line. If you're desperately grasping for something worth holding on to, try and take a few steps out the front door: move away from the depressing TV and the phone. Try and go a little further each day and, when you fail to achieve this sometimes, know in advance that you will and accept this, accept this failing while being fully aware that it doesn't matter. We all have to take some steps forward knowing that at some point we also have to fall back. Life is not linear and to honour that we should do our best to accept that at times we have to go backwards. In fact, it is often good for us to go backwards in order to figure things out – to help 'unstick' ourselves – so that we can start moving forward once again, armed this time with a little more self-knowledge and understanding and a newly acquired sense of self-respect and grace.

And to those of you seeking hard to deal with your addictions, I encourage you also to try walking. Why, you ask? Because it is easier to leave something behind when we know we have something else to move or walk towards.

Many of us need a crutch at some time in our lives when we are most in need of support and emotional or mental relief. Initially, we may think that this crutch has to be something external, something outside of ourselves, and so turn to alcohol or drugs or something equally tangible and easy to get into, yet later so difficult to give up and leave behind. When we choose a crutch that is outside of ourselves, it is doomed to fail, to let us down. When we get to a solution that works, we always discover that the answer does (and always did) lie within but we have to figure this out for ourselves first. This means we have to actually live through it.

We all know at some level when we have to leave an addictive crutch behind because it's damaging our hearts, minds and souls (be it drugs, food, alcohol, gambling, damaging relationships or other) and sometimes, through the mere act of walking, we can become aware of those addictions and process them enough to formulate a workable solution to ease the addiction and eventually cut it out altogether. Walking takes us to the woods so we can see the trees. You can't get more real than that!

Walking can help lift us up and out of our traumas, our fixed sense of self and psyche. It can help us move into new realms - unchartered ways of being - that enable us to heal that recognisable, damaged part of ourselves that so desperately wants to be healed. And that's why I like discovering new terrain – not the same old, well-known and hard-trodden paths that we've walked down a million times before and know like the back of our hands – I want to travel through new terrain to discover new learnings about me. A new zest for life and so many reasons for living will inevitably follow.

In your initial forays, focus on every single footstep that you take, becoming aware of how it feels to place your foot on the earth. Notice how supported you are by the earth, how she absorbs your foot and holds you steady with each and every step. As you get more confident, thank the earth for supporting you each time you place your foot on her. Each time you raise your foot, try to feel stronger as the earth sends her own life energy pulsating up through your body, giving you strength and fuel enough to carry on. Thank the earth for helping you, for not judging you, for being the silent partner holding your hand, guiding you as you move forward on your own path to recovery.

Over time, the thanks become a natural reflex as do the sensations of being supported and loved by the earth. Your gratitude will grow as you develop your own strengths and come to discover your own personal truths. Not only will the earth whisper her secrets to you but she will also help you uncover your own. Trust the earth and pour your heart and soul into her. The earth will pour her heart and soul into you.

Without trying to figure out how, just accept that one day the earth will show you how to become your own master. When this time comes, you will be living without fear. You will have come a long way down the road of self-healing.

Until that point comes, don't ask questions. When you go out to walk, focus on one foot after another and, when the questions come, ignore them. Focus on the earth. When questions, doubts, or fears arise, ignore them. Focus on the earth. The questions will get answered in their own way, their own place, when the right time comes. Trust the earth and focus on her. She will not let you down.

I spent the first half of my life running away from myself. I ran away to avoid meeting the real me. Now I choose to walk in order to meet myself again and again and through doing so, I've found out that I actually quite like me. Alongside learning the good, the bad and the ugly, I've come to better appreciate my life experiences and myself and thus am able to be more patient, accepting and loving of myself. Whereas in my early years if someone asked me what were my good qualities I would simply look blank, now I can happily list them.

I am no angel, nor have I ever been, but what I do find through walking is that I become more peaceful because walking helps me to become more of me. Out in the natural, green world, I find myself, and all the good and the bad about me and about everything else as well. Walking opens doors to life, to new thinking and new ways of being. It's a freeing experience and I love it. It enables me to face life without fear.

When I walk, I don't judge myself. I just walk myself into the present moment and, in this state of being, I can release all that would otherwise hold me back. When I do this, I am being truthful with myself. What I learn about myself and acknowledge - not deny - helps me to accept myself as I am. When I am truthful with myself it means I have nothing left to fear for, if I am not hiding from myself, I am not hiding from anyone else either. Nobody therefore can hurt me. Nobody can use anything against me. I have nothing to fear from myself or anyone else when I am singing my own truth. In this way, the truth sets me free.

Hills and mountains for me are not only symbolic metaphors but they also physically help us to remove the mountains of our minds. Simply put, if I want to clear my head, I go climb a hill or a mountain. When we exert ourselves through walking uphill, we pant with the required extra effort and this forces us to breathe more deeply and thus become more present in the moment. Climbing helps us to develop more patience because we are obliged to slow down, reducing speed and momentum in order to continue on our path. Slowing down allows us more time to see and feel the journey, to become the journey, so that we can start to enjoy the journey. Uphill, when we drive too hard it hurts and so we learn not to overly push it and to ease up a little instead. On life's journey, when we ease up a little we are showing ourselves loving kindness, acceptance of who and what we are and of our strengths and our limitations. Over time, we are capable of walking ourselves into acceptance of ourselves and eventually self-love. Given a little more time, we can all surely then learn to accept others and love them for the way they are too?

In my younger years, I spent much time being angry with people and feeling hard done by them when things went wrong or weren't working out quite right. I grew to distrust most people, feeling let down by them before I ever really knew them, and so kept myself at arm's length. I now know people didn't do anything to me. I did it all to myself. It was my own interpretation of events that harmed me. Since those days, I've walked my way into learning how important it is to take responsibility for my emotions, the way I feel, how I act and react, and to get on and be part of the human race without any notions of victimisation. For me, it would be too easy to find some remote place in the mountains where I could spend the rest of my life in peace and solitude and simply sidestep the issue of living alongside the rest of the human race. But, now I know how to listen to my instinct a little better, I see that this is not my true goal. My challenge, as it were, is to find my place within the human race. Being alone would just allow me to find peace within myself but that would only be half the journey, half the objective of my life's intended achievement. I have to find out how to participate in and serve better the human race and, to do that, it means I have to face up to all my fears.

When you go out walking in nature, the world reflects you back to you so that you see, hear and feel who and what you are. The natural world does not dilute you. Rather it flaunts you in all your magnificence and truth. When you participate at school, in the workplace, or in any other human-filled occupation, you become diluted. You have to let go of something, some part of you, in order to fit in and become what the role demands of you. It is not easy, therefore, to be part of the human world and, same time, maintain your unique, individual vibration. Nature, however, does not ask you to make that sacrifice. Nature just lets you be you. It is for this reason that I feel a need these days to consciously try to not let myself be diluted by the company of others. I spent the first half of my life living in fear of spending time alone, always running from me, afraid to uncover the real me. In the second half of my life, now that I've started to find out who I am and like it, I will continue to keep walking in order to discover how I can remain being me without diluting myself while in the company of others.

The Israeli Girl

Not so long ago, I was driving back from the supermarket when I saw a petite, young lady (in her early twenties perhaps, I'm no good at guessing ages) hitch-hiking alone. I often stop to pick up couples or men hitching on their own but I've never before seen a solo female hitchhiker. I stopped for her and soon learned that while she spoke English it wasn't her mother tongue and so I asked her where she was from. Israel came back the reply. She apparently flew into Spain, spent a few weeks discovering that side of the Pyrenees, and then crossed the border to explore the French side for the remainder of her summer holidays. She walked (or hitch-hiked) everywhere under the weight of the biggest backpack I have ever seen.

Her English was stilted but good enough for us to converse easily. However, it was her body language that spoke to me the loudest. This young lady was just so excited about everything she saw. She marvelled at the vivid colour and vast quantity of bright, yellow sunflowers dancing in the fields as we drove past. She gazed up in awe at the blueness of the cloudless sky overhead; she smelt the richness of the dense and ancient greens of the forest; and she really did giggle when she saw the buzzards diving and swooping low past the car and the donkeys grazing in the pastures. I looked at her and asked her what she was thinking and she simply bubbled over trying to explain to me the beauty in everything she saw and heard, felt and smelt around her. She lived in the desert, she said, and was not accustomed to seeing such vibrant colours and such a diversity of life-forms all around her. She told me how, when she bivouacked at night in the forest she was fascinated by both the smallest and biggest of creatures she encountered because they were so different to back home. I got the deep impression that she was quite literally high on loving it all.

And I smiled and my heart soared as I realised that I was bearing witness to another young soul walking fearlessly into her own destiny of freedom. Here was a young sapling of a woman, out on her own, in a foreign country where she couldn't speak the language and neither was she concerned about it. She was travelling with no fear, an absolute love of life and utterly drunk on the beauty of the natural world around her. This young Israeli woman was nothing but grateful for the experience, had no worries or concerns and thus no fears. Beauty was in everything she saw and experienced and, when my turn-off came and I dropped her at the roadside, I pulled away in the car believing absolutely that the universe would be generous and look after and protect this very special person throughout her joyous life.

It also reminded me that it is wrong to teach young pups the tricks of older dogs. When we do, we stymie their learning, growth and evolution. Worse, we instil them with our fears and worries and that's just downright mean.

Spending time outside in the living, green world, filling my senses with the beauty of everything that nature offers, I have learned how to reconnect myself as part of the natural world. In detaching myself from the man-made, technology-mad towns and cities, I find myself effortlessly moving more harmoniously with nature. This explains how I can experience so many interactions with animals and insects without them fearing me. As I become more in tune with my natural state, I move in tune with the pace of the natural world around me, and everything living and breathing in that space knows that. They can now read me, as it were, because I have become something they understand as I now resonate on a more natural frequency. They sense that there is no reason to fear me, I am no predator, and so they reveal themselves to me as if to share a part of their life story with me. Reciprocally, I have no fear of them because I know (presumably in the same way they know) that they intend me no harm.

I have also discovered what helps me determine the difference between being stupid and paranoid. When I am out there and more in touch with nature and my natural state, I listen better to my body's reactions or gut instinct. When I start to move in harmony with my surroundings, I can detect (know or sense) when there is a very real and present danger and when my mind is simply playing out its own paranoid delusions. I can quite literally *feel* the difference. I assume that the absence of distractions (such as mobile phones) enables me to take greater notice of what is truly happening around me.

To clarify perhaps by example, I had been walking through my local woods one day when I decided to sit down and rest for a while on a raised mound at the junction of where two trails crossed. I closed my eyes and lay back on the earth, enjoying the warmth of the sun's rays. It was a perfect moment. I was quite content to stay for a while but I suddenly became aware that the hairs on my arms had begun to stand on end and I felt as though the air had even chilled down a little. I looked around, certain that there were eyes upon me, but I saw no one. I closed my eyes again and tried to get back into the earlier, peaceful moment. But there had been a tangible shift in the energies around me; everything felt a little cooler and quieter now. In fact, the atmosphere felt *too* still. I then heard a plaintive cry in the undergrowth behind me and turned to see what it might be. The cry came again: once, twice, and so, on the third time, I stood up and turned towards it knowing full well that something wanted me to walk that way. It was that sort of a call. So I did. I got up and walked about fifty metres as close as I could to what I considered to be the source of the cry and – yes – it stopped by the time I got there. I mooched around for a short while scanning the undergrowth but I instinctively knew that I would never find the source of the cry. Since the peace of my restful moment had now been broken, I decided to continue on my way. A few short steps further and I pulled up suddenly, instinctively once again, and turned to where I had been sat just a few minutes earlier. Through a gap in the undergrowth, I spotted a wolf sniffing the mound and the air around where I'd been seated and I marvelled at the sight of this majestic animal. I reached for my camera and, as I stared at him, he turned to lock eyes with mine and I unflinchingly snapped a full, head-on, facial shot. We eyed each other for perhaps a full minute more before he seemingly made a decision and carried on his way. It was then that I saw yet another similar-sized wolf follow him and in between there were three small cubs, all black, all looking for food.

Something had urged me to move from that mound, of that I have no doubt. Instinct? Being in harmony with the natural world and its energies? Over-arching, guiding, universal energies protecting me? I say now, all of these. But I argue also that I could *hear* and just *know* what to do to remove myself from a potentially dangerous situation because I had an absolute, absence of fear. At no moment was I afraid. At no time did my mind kick in with a fearful and terrifying scenario of what might have been. I was free of fear and thus free to listen and feel, take note and act, to simply know and react. Being in harmony with the natural world had allowed the universal energies to communicate precisely what they needed to because I was not blocking them.

The natural world is my healing tank, my refuge, my home and, I've said before, my only religion is walking. Walking in this divine place and space makes me reverent, keeps me humble and sincere. Here I am at peace and, when I have inner peace, I can only be emanating greater peace to all around me too. If everyone went out for a walk and found peace, the world would be an entirely different place, wouldn't it?

If you have not already experienced it yourself, I would hope that after reading this book you will feel compelled to go for a long walk – by yourself - so that you may gain your own insights, reflections, inner peace and freedom. And I'm not just talking about a three hour circuit in the nearby hills. Go try your own Camino. Do a pilgrimage or long trek because you will benefit from it. Removing yourself from your everyday life, finding your own rhythmic pace and walking yourself into a virtual

meditative space, breathing in the beauty of the natural world instead of the cloying grime of the city: these all bring so much opportunity to unburden yourself, uncover the real you, and re-establish how you want to live your life. Caminos and long treks give you back to yourself. You give yourself permission to find yourself and take control once again. You too can find your freedom and happiness without fear. So go try it. Go walk alone.

I said that I am no angel. But, actually, I know now that I am. We all do right and we all do wrong but the important thing is that we grow to know who and what we are and learn from it. I don't mean any harm to anyone or anything and I am happy with who and what I am. And I'll keep walking as long as I can because it helps me reassert that feeling of happiness. It reminds me every time I go out that there's a reason to be grateful to be alive. I feel genuine gratitude out there looking at all there is in the natural world. It opens my heart, lifts my spirit and makes me smile. What more do we want from life than freedom and happiness and the absolute, absence of fear?

"Beware; for I am fearless, and therefore powerful."

.../...

195

Printed in Great
Britain
by Amazon

31771852R00112